PROBLEMS OF
SCHOLARLY PUBLICATION
IN THE HUMANITIES
AND SOCIAL SCIENCES

Problems of
Scholarly Publication
in the Humanities
and Social Sciences

A Report Prepared for the Committee on Scholarly

Publication of the American Council of Learned Societies

by RUSH WELTER

AMERICAN COUNCIL OF LEARNED SOCIETIES

New York

Library of Congress Catalog Card Number 59–11507

Printed and bound by the Plimpton Press, Norwood, Mass.

PRINTED IN THE UNITED STATES OF AMERICA

Table of Contents

Preface

This report represents an intensive effort on the part of the American Council of Learned Societies to find out what the problems of scholarly publication are in the humanities and social sciences, and what may be done to solve them. Therefore, and although I have had the main responsibility for formulating questions and interpreting the answers, the description of contemporary publishing that is presented here has drawn on the expert advice and assistance of a large number of individuals, each of whom contributed in no small measure to the success of the inquiry. Above all, it has benefited from the constant interest of the chairman and the members of the ACLS Committee on Scholarly Publication. It has also depended heavily on the guidance (and often the hard work) of other persons associated with the ACLS: Charlotte Bowman and Robert Hoopes of the New York office, faculty members scattered through the United States who are Regional Associates of the Council, and Howard Mumford Jones and Whitney J. Oates of its Board of Directors. Nor would this report have been possible without the cordial help of the many individuals to whom I turned for specific advice and information about publishing—not only those who responded, in their capacities as scholars or publishers or editors or teachers or librarians or administrators to my importunate questionnaires and interviews, but also those who went out of their way to introduce me to their scholarly communities or to help me to see more clearly what a publishing problem is and why it exists. I cannot name them individually, but I hope that they will not be disappointed by what has been made of their suggestions and observations.

This is, perhaps, an impossible hope. The problem of scholarly publishing is itself a most intricate problem in scholarship, and it touches areas of strong feeling if not partisan spirit. Hence

I cannot suppose that anyone who has not been through each of the stages of this inquiry will be willing to accept all of its conclusions in the terms in which they are stated. Nor should he do so if the argument that supports them seems inconclusive; yet I suggest that usable evidence is not so easily come by in this field of inquiry, and that (apart from certain unavoidable gaps) the present report takes into account as many of the aspects of scholarly publishing as it can and still proceed to a conclusion. Granting much to scholars for the sake of scholarship, it nevertheless assumes that they must take the world as they find it, and it views the problem of scholarly publication as at once a scholarly and a practical question. Perhaps the only other indication of my own perspective I can offer is to say that were I to approach the problem all over again, I know that I should change some of the techniques of the inquiry but I am sure that the results would remain substantially what they are here.

RUSH WELTER

Bennington College
March 1, 1959

Introduction

The publication of the results of scholarly research is an integral part of the process by which learning is advanced. A scholar has not only the desire but the responsibility to submit the results of his inquiries to the judgment of his peers and to as wide an interested audience as possible. All universities and colleges take pride in the publications of their faculty members, and in many of them publication is a major criterion for promotion and tenure. This attitude is so general that among scholars one frequently hears of complaints about policies of "publish or perish" or, more mildly, the "pressure to publish."

The American Council of Learned Societies, which administers a number of programs directed toward the support of scholarly research, felt that there was a need for a thorough study of the publication problems which confront the scholar. Rather than investigate the "pressure to publish," however, the Council judged that it would be more useful, and more amenable to objective inquiry, to determine whether or not scholarly works face difficulties which are extrinsic to their scholarly merit, in attaining publication in journals or books. Even before the study was begun we assumed that the economics of publishing nowadays make commercial publication unprofitable for most scholarly manuscripts. We also assumed that the present publication media for scholarship depend heavily on subsidies, both direct and indirect, from universities, foundations, and scholars. Both of these assumptions were borne out by our study. Our questions were directed at finding how large a problem remained despite the considerable support from all sources which makes possible the publication of about 725 books and a much larger number of articles a year in the humanities and social sciences.

There are scholars who feel that publication is the main problem of scholarship today. From them one gets the vision of mountainous stacks of manuscripts, unpublished for lack of money to get them into print.

Publishers, on the other hand, can be found who will state categorically that no good scholarly manuscript fails of publication today, that they are looking for manuscripts, that scholars do not know how to write, and so on.

What are the facts?

This report is the result of a year's effort to find them. Since the Council exists to serve scholars, we were frankly looking for evidence of scholarly difficulties, but we wanted evidence, not hearsay.

The first step, taken in the fall of 1957, was to appoint a Committee on Scholarly Publication, made up of three commercial publishers (Thomas A. Bledsoe, William Jovanovich, and Victor Weybright), three university press directors (Bernard B. Perry, Victor Reynolds, and Roger W. Shugg), and three scholars (Erwin R. Goodenough, Archibald A. Hill, and Joseph R. Strayer), with the undersigned as chairman.

To find the facts, the Committee proposed an extensive inquiry into the publishing experience of individual scholars, the publishing practice of commercial and university presses and of learned journals, the attitudes toward publication of college and university administrators, and the experience and views of other specialists who might be expected to cast light on contemporary publishing.

Rush Welter, on leave from his post as professor of the History of American Civilization at Bennington College, was placed in charge of the investigation. This report was written by him for the Committee. It is published with the unanimous support of the members.

I stress this unanimity because it represents a year-long process of education. At its first meeting, the Committee found that its members held widely differing views. It was clear from the outset that the problem of scholarly publication was above all else a problem of sharply divergent perspectives. As the report shows, many interests are at stake and many considerations enter into the publication of scholarly manuscripts—too many to permit even experienced scholars or editors or publishers to state conclusively what the problem really is. The report thus presents findings that will be questioned by different authorities speaking from different perspectives. Nonetheless, the members of the Committee, as a result of their meetings and their consideration of the results of the study, now agree in finding the conclusions plausible and take the responsibility for their publication.

The inquiry was designed to provide testimony from all parties involved in the problem. Questionnaires were sent to scholars, editors of learned journals, and to directors of university presses. Interviews were conducted in several regions of the country with commercial publishers, university press directors and staff members, faculty members of university press committees, editors of learned journals, college and university presidents and deans and heads of departments, experienced scholars, and spokesmen for college and university research councils, college and university libraries, graduate library schools, learned societies, and philanthropic foundations.

Our questionnaires were extensive, and required no little time and labor to answer. We are especially appreciative of the cooperation we received from the press directors, journal editors, and individual scholars in filling what must have been for many of them a burdensome request. The hundreds of other individuals who participated in the study were equally generous with their time and information.

We wish also to express our thanks to the United States Steel Foundation for a grant which will cover the cost of printing this report (thus insuring that it does not become yet another publication problem) and to Harcourt, Brace and Company for a contribution toward the expenses of the study.

This does not claim to be a definitive survey in the statistical or scientific sense. We did not have the means to make such a survey, even if, as some of us doubt, the problem lends itself to such analysis. In any event, it is our considered opinion that, in these pages, Dr. Welter has provided the most extensive and best attested view of the problems of scholarly publication available today.

FREDERICK BURKHARDT, Chairman
Committee on Scholarly Publication
American Council of Learned Societies

PROBLEMS OF
SCHOLARLY PUBLICATION
IN THE HUMANITIES
AND SOCIAL SCIENCES

1.

The Publishing Experience of Scholars

The first stage of our inquiry was an attempt to gather specific information about the recent publishing experience of scholars in the humanities and social sciences. For this purpose we made use of an elaborate questionnaire, directed to some 2200 faculty members in American colleges and universities, who were asked to report in detail the history of each of their manuscripts that had been accepted or rejected for publication during 1955–1957. We knew that we could not reach a conclusive statement of the problems of scholarly publication by this means, if only because the Ford Foundation grants to university presses postdated most of the period for which we sought detailed information, but we hoped that the answers scholars provided would serve to amplify the descriptions of publication and of publishing problems that we knew would become available to us through interviews and correspondence with experienced scholars, administrators, and editors.[1]

Because we had already planned a number of interviews with distinguished scholars, we solicited answers to our questionnaire only from faculty members below the rank of full professor. In some cases, moreover, we used faculty members in a single field of study as representatives for scholars in several allied fields either because, like French, the single field seemed typical or be-

[1] In 1957 the Ford Foundation announced an appropriation of $1,725,-000 for grants to American university presses, to be awarded over a five-year period, in support of book publication in the humanities and social sciences. Grants have been made to thirty-two university presses and during the first two years of the program funds have been allocated for the publication of approximately 287 titles in addition to the normal output of the participating presses. It is a condition of the grant that at least 50 per cent of the Foundation funds must be used in the publication of manuscripts submitted by authors outside of institutions affiliated with a press eligible to receive a grant.

cause, like Classics or Arts, it gave us access to a wider range of scholarship through the academic channels that were most open to us.[2] Operating within these limits, we asked deans and heads of departments (deans in small colleges and universities, heads of departments in larger institutions) in seventy-nine colleges and universities to request active scholars of appropriate rank who were also full-time members of the faculty in any one of nine fields of scholarship (English and American Literature, French Language and Literature, Classics, European and American History, Philosophy, History and Theory of Art, History and Theory of Music, Geography, and Political Science) to fill out our questionnaires.[3] After ten weeks we followed the original letter with another, telling each dean and head of department which faculty members had responded and requesting that he urge others to reply as soon as possible. We also asked how many questionnaires each dean or chairman had actually distributed, and gave him an opportunity to ask for additional copies, as a number did. The responses we received during a period of six months provide the basis for this section of our report.

In distributing questionnaires to a relatively broad sample of individual scholars we expected to elicit particular examples of publishing difficulties, but the relatively small number of replies we received provided few examples of publication deferred or refused.[4] Grouping all nine fields of scholarship together, and total-

[2] In addition it should be said that we passed over scholars in Anthropology and related fields because of the American Anthropological Association's recent investigation of publication; and we undertook only an abbreviated inquiry into the experience of economists because of our belief (validated by our results) that in general the problems of scholarly publication in Economics are less severe than those in any of the fields we investigated more extensively.

[3] Deans and heads of departments were asked to distribute the questionnaire to "every person who carries on scholarly research in his field, whether or not he regularly publishes."

[4] In circulating questionnaires we assumed that most scholars who had experienced publication difficulties during the years under consideration would be willing to report in detail the information we requested concerning their manuscripts, and that failure to reply would indicate an absence of serious problems. It now seems likely that many scholars were reluctant to complete the questionnaire despite its sponsorship and its purposes. It is probably significant, for example, that the responses received after our follow-up letter to deans and heads of departments reported a somewhat lower rate of acceptances than those received before it.

4

ing indiscriminately all scholarly manuscripts intended for publication in book form, we find that 82 per cent of 249 manuscripts reported submitted for editorial consideration during 1955–1957 were accepted for publication, 72 per cent without requiring that the author contribute any part of the cost of publication. The comparable figures for volumes reporting the results of scholarly research were 71 per cent and 57 per cent. (Here and elsewhere in this discussion book manuscripts accepted but awaiting a subvention when the questionnaire was returned are grouped with those already published partly or wholly at the author's expense, although in some instances publishers who have accepted manuscripts still awaiting subsidy would probably refuse a subvention from an author's personal funds.) During the same three years, moreover, 84 per cent of 738 articles reported were accepted for publication, all but a handful without financial contribution from the author.[5]

We know, however, that even in general terms these figures present a misleading picture of scholarly publishing today, if only because (as publishers and editors demonstrated in their answers to another of our questionnaires) nothing like 80 per cent of submitted manuscripts are accepted for publication, and because our presses certainly do not publish as many volumes in the humanities and social sciences as a simple extrapolation from these fig-

---

The fact remains, however, that selected scholars were given an unprecedented opportunity to report problems of publication, and that relatively few individuals did so. We have responses from only 479 faculty members of appropriate ranks and departments, which constitute 25 per cent of the questionnaires that may have reached appropriate faculty members, and 29 per cent of those that may have reached appropriate faculty members in institutions or departments known to have responded in some fashion, if only by letter, to our inquiry. We also have responses from 74 economists, 79 full professors, and 72 faculty members representing fields of scholarship not surveyed by means of the questionnaire.

[5] Scholars were asked to report scholarly manuscripts accepted for publication without contingency, those accepted for publication but awaiting a subsidy, and those not accepted for publication, during 1955–1957, together with the basic facts of their academic careers (including the dates, topics, and publishing fates of their successive dissertations) and certain other matters bearing on the policies and attitudes of their respective institutions toward publication and research.

A tabulation of the data we have on scholarly manuscripts will be found in Appendices A and B.

ures would suggest.[6] But we also know a good deal about the conditions that governed our approach to scholarly authors, and we infer that we have acquired a useful perspective on the experience of a small number of successful and moderately successful scholars, whose experience becomes that much more suggestive wherever it points to unsolved problems.

For one thing, in devising our sample of scholars we made use of a carefully designed list of colleges and universities employed by the College Department of a prominent trade publishing house in estimating potential demand for college textbooks, a list that includes every type of institution from large public or private university to small denominational college. But in order to insure that we understood the problems of publication affecting scholars in institutions of major rank and reputation (where we had reason to believe that the pressure to publish is more severe), we weighted this basic list by adding to it a small number of colleges and universities of high prestige. As it turned out, the returns from these additional institutions reported a considerably greater number of manuscripts per scholar than those on the original list, but demonstrated no decisive advantage in acceptances. Hence our modification of the original sample, while it exaggerated the productivity of American scholars, had chiefly the effect of increasing the number of manuscripts on which we have information, and it did not significantly alter the patterns of publishing experience in which we were primarily interested.

In certain other respects our sampling procedure probably had a greater influence on the proportion of manuscripts reported accepted by responsive scholars. For one thing, deans and heads of departments may have chosen to approach only the more successful members of their faculties, while in turn only the more successful individuals who received questionnaires may have filled them out. Furthermore, most scholars reported only acceptances in the case of successful manuscripts, excluding from their data an unstated number of prior submissions that would have changed the apparent ratio between acceptances and submissions although it would not have affected the ultimate status of individual manuscripts. Finally, it is impossible to count what scholars may have

[6] The editors' replies will be discussed in the second chapter of this report.

forgotten to put down, or to rectify errors they may have made in reporting the publishing fate of their manuscripts. There was room for error at every stage of the investigation, and it will not do to take the results of the questionnaires literally.

Yet despite these obvious drawbacks the scholars' responses can go far toward illuminating many of the difficulties that affect scholarly publication today. For while we undoubtedly received a disproportionate number of replies from productive and successful authors, the productivity they reported does not seem extreme, and their very number offers some assurance that their experience is significant.[7] Moreover, if we assume, cautiously, that our responses represent the experience of no more than 29 per cent of the individuals who received questionnaires, we find nonetheless that the proportion of responses to the number of questionnaires presumed to have been distributed varies directly with the prestige of the institutions polled.[8] One would not venture on this basis to "prove" that we have representative responses even from prestigious institutions, but certainly it seems plausible that the most productive scholars are likely to be teaching in the best-known institutions, and that we have an excellent perspective on their experience.[9]

[7] The 479 scholars in our sample reported an average of only one-half of one book manuscript apiece, and only one-fourth of one full-length volume embodying the results of original research, during the three-year period; and simultaneously they reported an average of less than two manuscripts of scholarly articles.

[8] Dividing thirty large institutions into two groups according to their academic reputation, for instance, we find that 33 per cent of the 792 scholars in institutions of higher rank who may be presumed to have received questionnaires, but only 22 per cent of 430 scholars in institutions of lesser rank, returned them. Dividing the smaller institutions into two groups reveals a similar discrepancy.

Because of the nature of our sample the difficulty that might be expected to arise in ranking thirty institutions of higher learning is almost nonexistent. Difficulties do arise in attempting to distinguish among institutions within either group, but even here they are not overwhelming, and such ranking extends the pattern that is described. Granting for the purposes of argument the accuracy of our rating, the top seven institutions returned 39 per cent of their questionnaires, while the next eight returned only 29 per cent.

[9] There is a good deal of incidental support for this view in our tabulation of scholars' responses to our request that they "characterize the policy of your department and your institution with respect to scholarly publication" insofar as it makes publication "essential, desirable, or useful for securing promotions, tenure appointments, or salary raises." Scholars in the

In many respects, then, the results of the questionnaires are inconclusive; but they still tell us a good deal about contemporary scholarship and its problems. Above all, they may be taken as indications of what is a publishing problem even if they cannot prove what is not, and if we pass by the absolute figures in order to study their internal relationships, as for instance by measuring the comparative successes of different kinds of manuscripts, we may discover hints of troubles that will help confirm the informal and usually nonquantitative judgments expressed in interviews and correspondence.[10]

One of the circumstances that may well cause us some concern, for example, is the fact that more than a year after the first Ford grants to university presses we learned that thirteen book manuscripts, otherwise approved and accepted, still awaited subsidy as a condition of publication. Moreover, a majority of these manuscripts consisted of full-length volumes embodying the results of original research. The figures are too small to permit conclusive inferences, but they suggest that publication of a volume of original research, which is the primary vehicle of scholarly communication in many fields, may too often depend upon the good fortune of the author in finding or providing funds to cover part or all of the cost of production, and the fact that most of the books reported published with the aid of an author's subvention

---

two fields of study (English and American Literature and History) from which we have the largest number of returns made clear that in seven large institutions of the highest rank publication is generally considered essential to all three; that in eight institutions of the second rank it seems essential for tenure but more often desirable than essential for promotions and raises; and that in fifteen of the third rank it seems desirable or useful rather than essential to any of them.

[10] Of course no statistics can prove that any given manuscript should have been published; and for that matter the returns we have suggest that some unsuccessful authors were not so persistent as they might have been in seeking to publish difficult manuscripts, inasmuch as the average number of submissions reported for rejected book manuscripts is less than two. Yet the fact remains that 18 per cent of book manuscripts reported, and a larger proportion of volumes of research, went unpublished during 1955–1957.

In pursuing the comparative fates of different kinds of manuscript, of course, we must recognize once again the possibilities of error or misinformation in the scholars' responses to our questions. It is worth noting, however, that so far as we can tell most scholars who replied understood that the facts of their publishing experience were solicited impersonally and as objective examples of scholars' experience generally.

were research volumes of this sort only reinforces the suggestion.[11] Indeed the fact that independent volumes of original research fared less well than other categories of "book" manuscript may have large implications that a reported rate of acceptance of 71 per cent simply does not reveal.

Another evidence of difficulties appears in the fact that a number of scholarly manuscripts found acceptance by foreign rather than domestic publishers, a circumstance that reduces the rate of domestic acceptances without personal subvention or contingency of subsidy (stated as a proportion of all submissions here and abroad) to as few as 64 per cent of all book manuscripts and 51 per cent of volumes of original research. Although some manuscripts undoubtedly reached appropriate publication in Europe, it is at least arguable that if they were publishable there they should have been able to find publication in the United States, and it is clear that in a number of instances scholars resorted to publication abroad only because they could not achieve it here.

Finally, it may be noted that manuscripts apparently derived from doctoral dissertations fared less well than other manuscripts, although of course subtracting them from our inclusive figures has the effect of raising the rates of acceptance reported for other kinds of manuscripts.[12] The differences do not seem extraordinary, given the fact that many young scholars attempt publication of their theses almost automatically; and the figures on full-length volumes of original research accepted without subsidy by domestic publishers, where one might have expected the most striking discrepancy to appear, show a relatively small difference between dissertation-derived and other types of manuscript. Yet there are significant statistical differences, especially in manuscripts accepted without personal subvention or contingency of subsidy, and it will not do to disregard them simply because doctoral disserta-

[11] In this context it is also significant that of twenty subsidies reported to have been provided by scholarly authors or solicited by bona fide publishing houses, only six of the eleven amounting to less than $1500 involved full-length volumes of research, as compared with seven out of the nine amounting to more than $1500. (The size of five other subsidies paid or solicited, including four on behalf of volumes of research, is not given.)

[12] The exact proportions on which the statements made above are based are presented in the following table, in which "Total acceptances" exclude domestic vanity-press acceptances but include titles for which authors supplied a subvention or for which publication waits upon a subsidy of some

tions are generally reputed to be "unpublishable." Perhaps they are; but our figures can do no more than confirm the belief that many fail of publication, and encourage us to explore the reasons in an appropriate place.

Meanwhile the scholars' replies to our questionnaire offer us persuasive statistical evidence of publishing difficulties affecting separate fields of study. Granted that proportions and percentages cannot be treated as conclusive in fields that are represented by only a few returns, there is good reason to consider the events they describe as useful clues to problem areas. For example, eighteen replies in Art are not a landslide; but in comparison with replies in other fields they suggest that acceptances of book manuscripts too often depended upon special circumstances like personal subvention and foreign publication, and they identify two manuscripts that were not accepted on any terms. In a small field of scholarship like the History and Theory of Art even a few examples may well indicate the existence of genuine difficulties in book publication, especially when one keeps in mind that rejections may reflect the high cost of art publication and not merely the poor quality of some manuscripts.

By the same token, analyzing the number of acceptances based upon actual or implied author subsidy in each of the other

---

sort. "Acceptances without subsidy" are those neither involving an author's personal funds nor contingent upon receipt of a subsidy.

	All Mss.	All Except Ph.D. Mss.	Ph.D. Mss.
Total acceptances of 249 Mss. of all types	82%	88%	73%
Acceptances without subsidy	72	81	56
Total domestic acceptances of 249 Mss. of all types (percentage of all submissions)	73	76	66
Acceptances without subsidy	64	70	53
Total acceptances of 120 full-length volumes of research among the above	71	78	66
Acceptances without subsidy	57	70	47
Total domestic acceptances of 120 full-length volumes of research among the above (percentage of all submissions)	63	66	61
Acceptances without subsidy	51	58	46

fields of study from which we have returns (none of which reports an over-all rate of acceptance of less than 70 per cent of the book manuscripts submitted), we find that subsidies were demanded for the publication of a sizable number of manuscripts in English and American Literature and American History, and an even more disproportionate number in French and Music. At the same time the titles still awaiting subsidy were most numerous in English and American Literature and American History, although they were also well distributed among the fields for which we have information.[13] Again some of our figures are based upon a very small number of scholars' replies, yet they clearly suggest that some problems of publication remain to be solved, and they point to French and Music as small fields in which serious difficulties may exist.[14]

These inferences are reinforced by a consideration of the fate of independent volumes of original research in different fields of scholarship. While the over-all rate of acceptances for these manuscripts was lower than the rate of acceptances for all kinds of book manuscripts in most fields of study, the proportion of volumes of research accepted only on the basis of a personal subvention or contingent upon receipt of some form of subsidy was notably larger in English and American Literature and in Music than the proportion of all kinds of book manuscript accepted on that basis, and it was suggestively large also in American History and French. Further, two manuscripts each in English and American Literature and in American History, and one each in Political Science, French, and Music, still await subsidy. Hence there is evidence of a sort that at least in the fields of English and American Literature, American History, French, and Music the book-length manuscript embodying the results of original research confronts disproportionate obstacles to publication, although there are in-

---

[13] In Economics, seventy-four returns, chiefly from universities ranking in the first or second of our prestige groups, showed an acceptance of 98 per cent of forty-five manuscripts, 89 per cent without actual or implied subsidy by the author. Yet three of the four books accepted on the basis of a subsidy, all full-length volumes of original research, still awaited funds in excess of $1500 in 1958. (The amount of the author's subvention already provided for the fourth was not given.)

[14] Appendix A provides the data for these as for other inferences from the scholars' replies to their questionnaires.

dications that almost no field of study entirely escapes the special problems that this type of manuscript may create.

The scholars' answers to their questionnaires also suggest that the practice of publishing abroad is particularly common in certain areas of scholarship, especially Art, French, Geography, and Political Science. We have no reason to doubt that foreign publication may be appropriate for some kinds of work in certain fields of scholarship (for example, French Literature), and it is understandable that manuscripts in Art History and Geography should have found publication more convenient where the costs of composition and printing are generally lower than in the United States, but we cannot ignore the possibility that in all four fields publication abroad may in some instances have been an awkward alternative to domestic rejections or delays.[15]

The information we have on manuscripts derived from doctoral dissertations also points, though perhaps less clearly, to possible problem areas. Whereas manuscripts that appear to have been derived from theses fared relatively badly in Political Science and not much better in English and American Literature or Art, they actually fared equally well or better than other kinds of manuscript in European and American History, French, and Classics. (In Philosophy and Music all book manuscripts achieved acceptance on some terms; in Geography none was derived from a doctoral dissertation.) If we eliminate acceptances requiring subsidy we find that the basic pattern continues to hold true except in French and Music, where only a very small proportion of a small number of dissertation-derived manuscripts was accepted without the fact or the contingency of author subsidy. Hence if the figures we are using have significance they point toward special problems of dissertation publication in Political Science and English and American Literature, and, less surely, in French and Music. Of course they also serve to focus our more inclusive statements about subsidized manuscripts, which made publication in English and French and Music seem especially difficult.

Otherwise there are only a few situations that seem to have presented unusual difficulties to the scholars who replied to our

[15] The issue here is publication—not simply printing—abroad. Many domestic presses (and several learned journals) make use of European printers in order to reduce costs on difficult publication.

questionnaire. It may be significant, for instance, that the twenty-one edited texts that faculty members in English and American Literature reported, and the five prepared by scholars in French, had found significantly less acceptance either with or without subsidy than had similar volumes in other fields of scholarship; or that in American History, French, and Art a disproportionate number of such volumes required some form of subsidy in order to see print.

With this observation, however, we have reached the limits of the scholars' questionnaires in identifying possible problems of scholarly publishing today; and perhaps the surest lesson of all our statistics—a lesson that we must keep in mind as we turn to a consideration of the patterns of university press publishing in the United States—is that the circumstances of publication for any single manuscript may be much more complicated than a general description of contemporary publishing is likely to reveal.[16]

Nevertheless, and granting that it would be unwise to treat any of our inferences as a conclusive statement of publishing problems, we have established potentially valuable clues both to the special difficulties that may confront certain areas of scholarship and to the special types of manuscript that seem to create problems. Foreign publication and publication delayed pending receipt of subsidy both suggest that in spite of the general success of scholarly authors certain manuscripts are likely to confront unusual difficulties, while the disproportionate number of rejections of volumes of original research testifies that whatever these difficulties may be they often affect an important vehicle of scholarly communication. Of course a good many of the manuscripts that presented difficulties were apparently derived from doctoral dissertations, which may often be less deserving of publication than other kinds of study; yet we cannot simply disregard reported obstacles even in fields of scholarship in which they can probably

----

[16] No analysis of the returns concerning articles in learned journals is developed here because the rates of acceptance are so high—over 80 per cent of manuscripts submitted in every field of study but English and American Literature, which shows an acceptance of 77 per cent—and because there is so little evidence of problems connected with author subsidies or foreign publication or the publication of material drawn from doctoral dissertations.

The data on article manuscripts and publication will be found in Appendices A and B.

be accounted for in this fashion—much less in those fields in which manuscripts of nondissertation research suffered the greater proportion of rejections.

In any event, certain types of manuscripts, dissertation-derived or not, seem to have presented unusual problems to scholarly authors: primarily those requiring unduly expensive composition (illustrations, symbols, or foreign languages); secondarily, edited texts in the modern literatures and languages for which we have information. In addition there is evidence that uncomplicated manuscripts of original research in populous fields of scholarship (chiefly English and American Literature, but also Political Science and American History) found publication more difficult than did similar works in less crowded fields. If these hints of publication difficulties are borne out by our other inquiries we may begin to think that they are conclusive.

2.

The Publication of Scholarly Books

Rather than employ the results of the scholars' questionnaire directly, as hypotheses to be tested in the experience of university presses and university press spokesmen, we can make our best use of the information the presses have provided as another kind of perspective on contemporary publishing. In general the directors of university presses feel, as the scholars' replies seem at first glance to suggest, that there is no problem of scholarly publication today. But they too point to special kinds of problems that tend to qualify the optimism their general views reflect; and at the same time they speak of them in terms not of individual manuscripts but of types of manuscripts that create characteristic difficulties. Although their types are not identical with those that scholars reported either in their questionnaires or through other channels, because they are oriented to aspects of editing and manufacturing and distribution that do not immediately concern scholarly authors, in the long run they serve to extend and refine the scholars' complaints precisely because they refer to the actual process of publishing.[1] On the other hand editors neglect some of the problems that scholars describe, and this fact too makes a good reason for presenting them first of all in their own terms. Where there are differences in judgment between scholars and publishers they must be resolved through the use of all the kinds of data we can muster.[2]

[1] Nevertheless, this report, like the inquiry on which it is based, has deliberately ignored most technical problems affecting the manufacture and distribution of books, on the grounds that, in the first place, our main concern is manuscripts that should be published in spite of technical and financial problems and, secondly, that the Association of American University Presses is engaged in a study of manufacture, while distribution problems are being given consideration by the American Book Publishers' Council.

[2] In addition to the university presses we also approached eight commercial publishers for information and perspectives on the publication of

The data we have from the university presses consist of their formal responses to an elaborate questionnaire concerning their recent publishing experience, supplemented by direct personal contacts and informal correspondence. Forty-three university presses were asked to report as accurately as they could the number of scholarly titles published during a typical recent year, the number of manuscripts submitted and accepted or rejected at different stages of the review process, and the number, printings, sales, and royalties of volumes published with and without subsidy, together with a great deal of additional information both about manuscripts and published books and about the presses' experience and attitudes. Answering all these questions fully demanded extraordinary labors, especially on the part of large houses, but thirty-four presses replied in greater or lesser detail and twenty-eight provided complete or almost-complete answers.[3]

---

scholarly books. It soon became clear that while many of them are concerned as individuals over the fate of scholarly manuscripts they might once have found means to publish, they can hardly undertake now to solve problems of publication that university presses find difficult to deal with. Most of them continue to publish the kinds of scholarly book that seem to fit their lists, and some urged that trade presses not be automatically excluded from consideration as publishers of any volumes that may be sponsored by scholarly bodies, but their obvious good will cannot guarantee the publication of many difficult books.

Moreover, two additional considerations militate against trade presses' being thought of as potential publishers for scholarly manuscripts. One is the fairly obvious and quite understandable fact that when they publish a volume that constitutes an original contribution to scholarship in its field they do so either because they think it will become a scholarly best-seller or because they hope that in later books the author will return a profit on their original investment. Occasionally, of course, a trade publisher accepts a book simply because he believes in it; but every such volume makes a powerful financial reason for not publishing others of its kind.

The other objection to trade publication of primarily scholarly works is the fact that university presses, which can break even on much smaller press runs than can commercial publishers, need profitable books to balance the losses they suffer on books that trade presses would not dream of publishing. Of course some trade publishers insist that university presses cannot or at least do not give their books the same publicity that trade titles receive, but although this argument may attract scholarly authors it cannot compensate for the long-term disadvantages to scholarship of trade publication of promising scholarly manuscripts.

Appendix B indicates the extent to which scholars responding to our questionnaire found publication for manuscripts with commercial presses.

[3] For a list of university presses that provided information see Appendix C. It was not always feasible for a press to answer all of our questions

The first point they made clear is the great number of scholarly volumes in the humanities and social sciences that American university presses publish. In a typical year just preceding the Ford Foundation grants to university presses, twenty-six houses put out 583 such titles. (Twenty-one of these presses reported a total of 594 books, of which they consider that 554, or 93 per cent, were scholarly, and 453, or 76 per cent of the total, titles in the humanities and social sciences.)[4] By estimating the number of volumes published by other houses on the basis of their known size and other factors we may conclude that even without the Ford grants all our presses could be expected to publish as many as 725

---

in the exact terms in which they were put. Sometimes the difficulty was one of incomplete records. Sometimes it was the impossibility even of estimating such matters as the number of years a title is expected to remain in stock, or the point at which it may be considered to have recovered both manufacturing and overhead costs. Often it arose from the necessity of proposing the same set of questions to every press, regardless of its special circumstances. Although we urged press directors to estimate as accurately as possible what they could not report precisely, and although we made every effort to pose questions that were flexible enough to fit different circumstances yet exact enough to solicit comparable data, the replies even from presses that cooperated wholeheartedly with the inquiry were not always usable, and sometimes we have been forced to exclude some of their figures from our tabulations.

Another special circumstance has also forced us to exclude some figures occasionally: that is, some anomalies were caused by minor discrepancies between an early questionnaire answered by four presses and the final draft of the same questions; and other anomalies arose out of the fact that in the final questionnaire we offered presses the option of giving us raw data in response to two questions instead of reporting answers derived from such data. In some few cases the results proved to be incompatible.

Answers to questions that are not discussed in the text will be found in Appendix D.

[4] Presses were asked to report actual figures for a recent normal year of scholarly publishing antedating the Ford grants or to report estimates for a hypothetical average year independent of the Ford grants. Twenty-nine presses chose to use actual figures (five for calendar or fiscal 1955, twelve for calendar or fiscal 1956, ten for calendar or fiscal 1957, and two for fiscal 1958), while three apparently reported hypothetical averages. In what follows data from all years have been averaged together except where, as in the figures above, the Ford grants may be presumed to have made a significant difference.

Quite apart from the Ford grants, however, a number of presses reported in answer to our question that their press runs and sales, and in some instances the number of manuscripts submitted, had been greater during 1957 than during the earlier year.

titles in the humanities and social sciences annually. Of course this gross figure makes no distinctions as to size or type of book (scholarly text, volume embodying the results of original research, short monograph, summary of contemporary scholarship, reprint of established scholarly title, volume published in conjunction with a foreign house, or even occasional experimental textbook), but, considered together with the range and variety of titles reported in the breakdown of volumes by printings and sales, it makes absolutely clear that American university publishing is both powerful and versatile.

It is equally clear that the editorial staffs and scholarly readers of these same presses carry out an extraordinary task in selecting manuscripts for publication. Although most of the press directors were able to do no more than estimate the number of manuscripts they had considered for publication during recent years, twenty-three who offered reasonably close approximations of the actual figures reported receiving 2389 manuscripts, of which they held 1480, or 62 per cent, for at least one extended reading by an editor or scholarly reader. Of these 1480 manuscripts 715, or 48 per cent, were retained for one or more additional readings, not to mention 125 that were returned with suggestions for revision and possible resubmission.[5]

Nor is the review procedure a simple or inexpensive one. Besides relying upon their own editorial staffs to make preliminary decisions about incoming manuscripts, most presses seek the expert advice of one or more recognized authorities in the field of scholarship appropriate to each manuscript that is seriously considered. When in doubt as to which authorities will provide the

[5] Ten presses from which we have what seems to have been an exact count of manuscripts submitted reported a total of 775 received, of which 583 (75 per cent) were retained for at least one extended reading, and of these 307 (53 per cent) were retained for additional readings. Significantly, the proportions between manuscripts submitted, manuscripts retained for one extended reading, and manuscripts retained for additional readings, vary hardly at all among two large presses, four middle-sized presses, and four small presses considered together in groups. (Here and elsewhere any press that reported publishing as many as thirty volumes during a single year counts as a large press, while a press that published between ten and thirty volumes counts as middle-sized and one that published ten or fewer counts as small. The number of presses providing usable data in each of these categories is nine, thirteen, and thirteen, respectively.)

best-qualified readings they solicit the advice of faculty members of the university or of its Press Committee; but for the most part established presses seem to feel that they have a good knowledge of the authorities in the fields in which they publish and that they know where to turn for impartial advice. Hence the only limitation on their free choice of readers is their tendency to select off-campus readers for manuscripts by members of their own faculties, and on-campus readers for manuscripts by outsiders.[6] Certainly they continue to employ much the same carefully designed procedures for the evaluation of manuscripts as are described in Chester Kerr's *Report on American University Presses*, published in 1949 by the Association of American University Presses.[7]

Manuscripts that satisfy both the press staff and its experts become eligible by that fact for publication; of the 715 scholarly manuscripts retained for more than one reading by the twenty-three presses from which we have reasonably accurate figures, 392 (or 55 per cent) were recommended for publication. Nevertheless, formal recommendations to publish must usually be confirmed by the press's governing body, and in rare instances an editorial recommendation will be reversed by this final authority.[8] On the other hand, seven of twenty-one presses that published titles in series reported 72 such volumes published without complete editorial discretion, presumably upon recommendation of a

[6] Some presses also report that in order to avoid potentially biased readings they solicit authors' opinions as to who would constitute an appropriate scholarly authority.

[7] The caution presses exercise, to the end that, in Kerr's words, they may "reduce the chances of publishing inferior manuscripts," explains in large measure the delays that seem to beset scholarly manuscripts under consideration for publication by university presses. According to eight presses of various sizes, the process of consideration for 62 per cent of 277 manuscripts kept for more than one extended reading occupied from three to six months, whereas the publishing fate of only 22 per cent was decided in less than three months' time. (In addition, 14 per cent of these manuscripts required from six to twelve months' consideration—and four took longer than twelve months.) Such figures as we have from other presses suggest, however, that unsuccessful manuscripts are usually rejected in a much shorter period of time.

[8] Of twenty-one editors who reported having recommended 432 manuscripts for publication, three reported having been reversed on a total of seven manuscripts. Six other editors did not respond to our question as to whether their governing boards had accepted their recommendations (a total of 192).

university department or faculty committee. The practice of non-discretionary publication is generally associated with the relatively inexpensive printing of monographs written by faculty members or graduate students of the publishing university, and most of it is concentrated in two large presses (which accounted for 56 such titles—36 of them doctoral dissertations that had been only slightly revised—out of the total of 72), but it is not peculiar to these few houses, and it suggests that even presses that exercise complete editorial discretion may occasionally find themselves publishing works they would not undertake if it were not for the existence of departmental or other special university subsidies.[9] Hence although departmental control over publication tends to incur the disapproval of directors of university presses, who feel that the criterion of worth is thereby threatened by such factors as faculty politics and faculty pride, the practice itself survives, and there is some indication that additional departments may acquire or revive the privilege in years to come.

Be that as it may, most university presses probably hope to provide especially well for the needs of their own faculties, although not to the extent of refusing to consider manuscripts from other sources on substantially competitive grounds. Indeed there was a tendency for large presses—except for the two reporting a large number of nondiscretionary titles in series—to publish fewer books by their own faculty members than smaller presses accepted; but there was also a fairly wide range of experience among different presses of roughly similar size.[10] Moreover, although four large presses as a group reported that 61 per cent of their titles repre-

[9] A total of nineteen presses reported receiving grants from departmental publication funds or other special appropriations from university sources during recent years.

[10] The figures from seven large presses show that 29 per cent of their titles had been written by members of their own faculties, as against 47 per cent of the titles published by twenty-three middle-sized and small presses. No large press reported more than 44 per cent of intramural titles, whereas eight out of thirteen middle-sized presses (and four out of ten small presses) reported at least that proportion.

The scholars' questionnaires also tell us something here. Among 72 book manuscripts published by American college and university presses during 1955–1957, some 55 were published by presses with which the scholars in question may be thought to have had some special familiarity, either as faculty members or as recipients of the doctoral degree. Of 38 book manuscripts apparently derived from their doctoral dissertations, moreover, schol-

sented unsolicited manuscripts, as against 76 per cent of the titles reported by sixteen lesser presses, almost the same proportions of their unsolicited titles (59 per cent as against 61 percent) had been submitted with intramural sponsorship. Clearly, contemporary patterns of university publishing suggest that scholarly authors often find publication with familiar or easily accessible presses congenial, but there is no reason to suppose from the data we have gathered that they find it indispensable.[11]

Whatever their relationships with members of the faculties of their own universities, most university presses survive only because of special appropriations and financial concessions made by the parent institutions to compensate for their economic difficulties. The Kerr Report suggests the nature and extent of these direct and indirect subsidies to university publishing. Our questionnaire, which elicited only scattered replies as to the amounts involved in various kinds of institutional subsidies, showed nevertheless that at least twenty out of thirty responsive presses received direct general subsidies from their parent institutions during given recent years, and that twenty-three received indirect concessions in such forms as free rent, utilities, storage, and maintenance. Lesser numbers of presses received other kinds of aid, including departmental appropriations for particular books (thirteen presses), special—rather than undifferentiated—university appropriations (thirteen presses), and below-cost use of working capital or manufacturing equipment (at least four presses).

---

ars found publication for 35 with familiar presses as against 3 with unfamiliar houses, whereas they found similar publication for only 20 out of 34 nondissertation manuscripts accepted. (These calculations include only full-length books—scholarly texts and translations as well as volumes of original research—accepted by presses associated with institutions of higher learning.)

[11] Of course these calculations apply to actual publication, and do not take into account the extent to which scholarly authors may first send their manuscripts to prestigious houses before turning to familiar or accessible presses. Nevertheless, the figures we have from fifteen large and middle-sized presses suggest that with certain unexpected exceptions, caused in part by variations in the processes of consideration, presses of almost every size and distinction accepted for publication surprisingly similar proportions of the manuscripts they retained for at least one extended reading. Seven presses, including what are probably four of the eight most distinguished university presses in the United States, and four of five such presses from which we have usable figures, report having accepted from 30 per cent to 40 per cent of manuscripts retained for one reading.

The chief reason for this dependence, which in several instances amounted to well over $100,000 for the year although in others it came to less than $10,000, was obviously the small sales potential of many of the books the presses undertook to publish. One indication of this sales potential is the first printings of volumes published upon a subvention, which seem to be based more often than not on the anticipated total sales of such titles. No less than 71 per cent of 212 such volumes reported by twenty-seven presses, which constituted 42 per cent of the total number of volumes published by these houses, were first printed in editions of less than 1801 copies, and no less than 49 per cent in editions of less than 1301. However low the break-even point (the number of sales at which a press recovers both manufacturing and overhead costs on a book) may be on scholarly volumes by comparison with trade titles, it is clear that it must be larger than 1800 copies for a great majority of volumes, and that the deficits incurred in scholarly publishing will be considerable. For that matter, twenty-one presses that replied to a further question reported that they expected to recover their own investment, exclusive of subvention, on at most 69 per cent of 137 volumes published upon subvention. The service that these presses provide to scholars both inside and outside their own universities constitutes a heavy burden on their operations, which can be made up only in part by their successes with titles of more general interest.[12]

Traditionally, of course, scholarly authors themselves have been asked to provide funds in support of publication when other resources have not been available. The Ford Foundation grants have made it possible for most presses to abandon authors' subventions except in special circumstances; but in fact rising costs of publication had already caused presses to look for other kinds of support even before the Ford Foundation grants had been initiated. During years immediately preceding the grants, for example, only nine of twenty-three presses from which we have data on this point solicited author subventions, in behalf of some 30 manu-

---

[12] The service that university presses provide in maintaining books in stock long after a commercial press would have remaindered them also constitutes a heavy financial burden that presses or their parent institutions must carry. Appendix D presents the data we have on this as on other aspects of university press publication.

scripts, of which approximately 10 had been accepted by a single press. In 19 cases (including all those involving the exigent press) these presses solicited author subsidies in amounts equal to the total subsidy required, as compared with 11 instances in which they sought amounts less than the total needed. The same nine presses, however, reported receiving personal subventions for only 24 manuscripts, including 8 at the exigent press. (In addition, four other presses reported receiving one unsolicited author subsidy apiece.) At the same time four of the ten presses that reported neither soliciting nor accepting author subsidies during the years under consideration received an unstated number of other subsidies to particular books or projects of the press. Clearly the commendable practice of sparing authors increases the need for other forms of subsidy.

Here, indeed, is unmistakable evidence of a problem of scholarly publication, which has been solved in part, and for a five-year period, by the generosity of the Ford Foundation. According to the majority of press directors with whom we were able to arrange personal interviews, the Ford grants have virtually eliminated the historic surplus of scholarly manuscripts. Yet at least two press spokesmen suggest that despite the Ford grants it will soon be necessary for them to solicit author subsidies or other additional funds, and several pointed out that Ford funds have had the effect rather of stimulating scholarly publishing in general than of providing all the financial support that scholarly books need today.[13] Be that as it may, of twenty-five presses that reported applying Ford funds to the publication of 112 scholarly books, twenty-two indicated that in the absence of other subsidies these grants made the difference between publication and rejection of as many as 68 manuscripts. Others suggested that it would be impossible to say that particular manuscripts had been published only because of Ford funds, which must be employed according to the formal specifications of the grants rather than where funds are most urgently needed at any given moment, but they made

[13] One press director feels that his press's grant has had the effect of drying up other nonuniversity sources of funds for the support of publication; but four presses, each of which received a Ford award, report increases in the funds available to them from within or without their universities.

clear nonetheless what a boon the grants have been. Furthermore, fourteen presses out of twenty-six replying to our question indicated that in recent years they had rejected at least 60 manuscripts that they would have published had additional funds been available, and three other presses reported an unidentified number of manuscripts in this category. Inasmuch as the Ford grants seem to many presses to have made "all the difference" in the last two years—although three Ford presses reported five manuscripts rejected for lack of funds since January 1957—if they come to an end in less than three years subsidy from other sources will be needed for many manuscripts.

At the same time many press directors have described critical problems in their current operations that this general discussion hardly touches. The difficulty the presses are most insistent or at least most numerous in describing is the book that requires disproportionately expensive composition. The normal scholarly manuscript in most fields, while it is costly by comparison with the average commercial product because of the need to include scholarly apparatus, is nonetheless reasonably cheaply converted into type. But the scholarly manuscript in such fields as Art History, Archaeology, Numismatics, and Anthropology usually depends for its effectiveness as a book upon the liberal inclusion of very expensive illustrative plates, while the typical manuscript in such disparate fields as Classical Philology, Musicology, the History of Science, Linguistics, and Economic Theory is all too likely to require difficult composition scattered through an entire volume. Philanthropic foundations have made funds available to cover the extraordinary costs of publishing in many of these fields, which generally suffer also from the lack of a large potential audience, but despite all efforts to raise additional funds and to economize on production costs the presses cannot see how they will be able to continue publishing such works indefinitely. For that matter economies are virtually impossible in the fields that cause the greatest anxiety, for while printing abroad and typewriter composition and even hand-lettering offer solutions for books in which the text creates added expenses there is no feasible way to economize on such materials as illustrative plates that does not threaten scholarship itself.

The next most critical problem that the press directors recognize is the scholarly tool that is not quite able to qualify as original scholarly research although its publication is essential to further scholarship—the translation of an important work available only in a foreign language, the annotated edition of a text already available in unsatisfactory form, the collection of important but inaccessible documents. Here it is not wholly clear where the presses would draw the line of scholarly necessity, for their answers to our questionnaire do not identify specific manuscripts or projects that have caused them difficulty, but there is a clear sense of urgency, and a widespread belief that funds should be made available to encourage scholars to work in these areas.

A number of press directors describe in equally compelling terms the problem of the long-term multivolume publishing venture, best exemplified recently by the Jefferson Papers, which found massive funds in support of the necessary scholarship but depended upon university press funds to achieve publication. As it happens, the Princeton University Press does not report that its commitment to this extraordinarily large enterprise constitutes a problem, but other presses have described equally significant projects (for example, publication of the La Follette Papers, which have never been printed, and reconstruction of the complete annals of the First Congress of the United States) that they have been unable to undertake because they could not tie up the necessary funds over a long period of time. Here the difficulty is probably less the expense of publication than the necessity of supporting such projects at every stage from scholarly preparation of the manuscript to the actual printing, but certainly the precedent of the Jefferson Papers cannot encourage any but the wealthiest presses, and there are more potential projects than there are potent publishers.[14]

The manuscript at the other extreme in size also causes difficulty for several presses. The economics of book publishing and distribution make almost any scholarly volume a difficult publishing venture, but they virtually prohibit the publication of

[14] Apparently encyclopedias and other large-scale reference works, although they are extraordinarily expensive to produce, confront fewer obstacles to publication itself. Their chief problem is to find funds that will cover the costs of original research and compilation, and when such expenses are provided for, the manuscript usually finds a commercial publisher.

works that run to less than 150 pages in print. Apparently in ordinary circumstances such a book cannot be priced at less than three dollars, and yet cannot be expected to sell even reasonably well at that seemingly high price. As a result a press has the alternatives of turning down the short manuscript outright despite its merits, of burying it in a larger volume containing several other essays, or of encouraging the writer to expand it beyond what the subject or his treatment requires. To be sure, presses do occasionally publish works of this sort in spite of their practical disadvantages, but the comments we have received clearly imply that they need financial help to do so.

Finally, a handful of press directors comment that the most debilitating publishing problem they confront is the impossibility of finding editorial time and energy and "publishing room" generally to perform all of the many tasks that truly effective scholarly publishing requires. The absence of sufficient resources, for example, forces them to turn away potentially interesting manuscripts because they cannot afford to spend time working them over with an author, even when as a novice he might thereby learn to be a more effective writer. It also interferes with their wish to engage in creative editing, which might encourage scholars to write about problems more broadly or more significantly than they traditionally have, and which might even make scholarship more effective by making it more interesting to the educated layman. In short, while they recognize that additional manufacturing funds are always useful to university presses, and that the Ford Foundation grants have expanded publishing opportunities, they believe that further achievements by the presses are blocked by a shortage of funds for editorial work, not manufacturing. This is a point of view seldom contemplated in discussions of the problems of scholarly publication.

In turn, of course, this press comment on the problem of editing scholarly manuscripts also amounts to a powerful indictment of the scholar as author. In fact a few press directors report themselves baffled by the ignorance scholarly writers display, and suggest that the absence of simple technical competence on scholars' part is a permanent condition rather than a problem worth trying to solve. On the other hand, approximately half of the press directors reported in answer to our questions that scholars all too frequently send their manuscripts to presses to which they are for various reasons inappropriate, while almost two-thirds complained that scholarly authors habitually ignore not only the standard rules for preparation of manuscripts available in such guides as the Chicago *Manual of Style* but also the elementary considerations of order, clarity, literacy, and consistency that should govern anything a scholar writes. (Some even complain that they are sent carbon copies of manuscripts, especially of doctoral dissertations, for editorial consideration.) The force of these criticisms is diminished somewhat by the fact that not all those who complained thought that better-prepared manuscripts would increase the speed or volume of their own publication, but there is no mistaking either the righteous wrath of many press spokesmen or the extreme culpability of many authors who should know better.

These, then, are the problems that university press directors in greater or lesser number describe. They clearly identify types of manuscripts that face unusual difficulties in reaching publication as books, and they also imply that certain adjustments would be desirable in the kinds of aid that philanthropic foundations are willing to offer to scholarship. Chiefly they suggest that while the Ford Foundation grants have been extraordinarily valuable for the support they have given to scholarly publishing generally, special funds are now required to provide support for purposes to which Ford funds are inappropriate if not actually ineligible. (No press is willing, for instance, to tie up all of its Ford grant in one or two special ventures, when it has a number of less expensive volumes that can be published for the same amount of money.) In particular they suggest that foundations which support research projects might take a greater responsibility for seeing results of the research into print. Customarily, foundations have been reluctant to provide publication for research they have sponsored lest they commit themselves in advance to unworthy manuscripts or, on the other hand, lest they seem to play the role of propagandist or partisan of the findings, and certainly no one would recommend that they make either mistake. But there is such a fault as being too conscious of virtue, at the expense of scholarship itself, and certainly there are areas of scholarly activity in which our evidence suggests that some agencies must play a larger supporting role if scholars are to remain productive.

27

On these points there is no disagreement between scholars and presses. In general, in fact, our scholarly sources state the case for additional funds even more sharply than the university presses. It is clear both from correspondence and from personal interviews with experienced scholars in various fields of inquiry that several kinds of books offer special obstacles to publication; and scholars also bear witness—as publishers cannot—to their own needs for such works in the performance of their tasks.

A number of scholars, for instance, report volumes accepted for publication by learned societies or university presses but waiting for a subsidy of some sort to cover extraordinary costs of composition or illustration. Moreover, an even greater number testify to a grave need for funds in support of scholarly tool works, a category scholars extend to include not only annotated editions and translations but also a whole range of bibliographies and finding lists and dictionaries that the press directors do not emphasize. Many such works also create extraordinarily difficult problems of manufacture, yet even those that are relatively simple to produce often confront difficulty in reaching publication, while there are a number of manuscripts that have so far failed of publication because their great size makes them a burden even when the cost per page does not. Finally, scholars insist even more strenuously than university press directors upon the difficulty of publishing short books. As they see it the problem is twofold: particular manuscripts face difficulties in reaching integral publication, although they may find publication in successive issues of scholarly journals; and experienced scholars, who might be counted upon to make use of the extended essay form, simply do not turn to it as frequently as they should. Nor does the rather speculative cast of this argument disqualify it even in the eyes of directors of university presses, several of whom referred to potential as well as actual short manuscripts as a problem in scholarly publishing.

Nevertheless, it is true that scholars are more often inclined than directors of university presses to describe potential as well as actual manuscripts as problems of scholarly publication. In the view of a number of experienced scholars, for example, valuable scholarly inquiries are often abandoned without a trace because of anticipated obstacles to publication. What to make of this statement presents a difficult problem of analysis. So far as systematic evidence goes, our poll of 2200 scholars turned up some 125 individuals who cited abandoned projects, but the figures are hardly conclusive either way: how, after all, can one weigh either the merits of a proposed investigation or the difficulties of publishing a manuscript that was never completed, much less prove that anticipated difficulties in publication were mainly responsible for its abandonment? Nevertheless, the fact that such a problem was mentioned not only in the responses to our faculty questionnaires, where such information was solicited, but also in our correspondence and our interviews should carry a certain weight, even though most scholars—including, obviously, those whose manuscripts have already created publishing problems—seem first to complete what they wish to work on and only then to attempt to find ways of publishing it. After all, there is at least a logical reason to suppose that the experienced scholar, whose work is most likely to be significant, will have learned not to attempt certain kinds of scholarly inquiry; and there is empirical evidence that some of them warn their students against beginning studies that are unlikely to find publication easy. At the very least we may conclude that every distinctive problem of scholarly publication has probably created its backlog of uncompleted manuscripts, which is to say that here as elsewhere criteria external to scholarship itself have sometimes controlled scholarly pursuits.

3.

The Publication of Books
with Small Potential Sale, and Related Problems

It is clear that the university presses cannot publish every work that meets their professional standards, nor carry out every worthy project that attracts their interest. At the same time there are indications that difficulties may confront manuscripts of scholarly books even in areas that the university presses do not stress, and there are experienced scholars who criticize the very criteria and procedures of the presses in the name of more effective scholarship. No matter how rancorous some of their criticisms occasionally become we cannot lightly dismiss them, for they represent extensive practical experience, not only in scholarship but also in the expert reading of manuscripts and in service upon press boards. Perhaps the process of recording some of them will demonstrate their relevance.

One of the criticisms experienced scholars have leveled against university press publishing is the inadequacy of press mechanisms for the review of manuscripts. On the whole their quarrel is with the boards of governors who are formally charged with making the final decisions for or against publication, but it also extends to the scholarly referees whose opinion is solicited on submitted manuscripts. On one hand, the argument runs, a board of governors is manifestly not competent to judge the issues of scholarship that come before it, for even if it turns to faculty representatives for advice they will not all be specialists in the field any given manuscript represents. On the other hand, this argument also holds that the two or three scholarly readings upon which a decision to publish or to reject is usually based do not always give satisfactory results. Scholars' judgments are preferable to editors', but scholars see only what is put before them by the editors, they are chosen by the editors, and in addition they may suffer such various faults as intellectual obtuseness, scholarly timidity, academic factionalism, and personal prejudice.

Presumably very little of this criticism may be taken seriously, not because it is invariably inaccurate, but because in the nature of the case any institution will have characteristic defects, and it is difficult to imagine a superior way of deciding what manuscripts should be published once it is conceded that not every manuscript should see print. Commentators can be found to urge that any literate report of scholarly research should be published (and for a variety of reasons ranging from the importance to scholarship of disseminating in more or less permanent form the results of any serious research, to the vocational or even the psychological significance of getting even marginal work into print), but there is a fairly widespread consensus on the part of scholars that the subject of a book should be significant, its research effective, and its writing economical and purposeful. Yet criticism of the review process may have a larger relevance to our inquiry than is at first glance apparent, for it points up the fact that mistakes can be made despite the system, and any mistake is by definition a problem in our terms. Certainly the presses try to safeguard every manuscript against predictably hostile readings, and many of them go out of their way to separate editorial from financial considerations, but it is clear that they are unlikely to give a manuscript the benefit of the doubt when the deliberations of editors and readers are inconclusive.[1]

Moreover, scholarly critics suggest that some kinds of mistakes are inevitable because of the criteria that presses habitually apply to scholarly manuscripts, particularly the criterion of what makes a "book" rather than the criterion of what is useful to scholarship. According to these critics, the form a report on original research takes is far less important to other scholars than the availability of the material it has consolidated; yet most university presses are interested chiefly in what can be stated in an effectively dramatic pattern. By the same token they tend to publish only finished

[1] There is some evidence in the replies of university press directors to our press questionnaire, incidentally, that the manuscripts that require the longest period for consideration are those that may ultimately be rejected because of this kind of doubt on the part of a press. In this sense prolonged consideration amounts to an attempt to give the manuscript every chance.

and conclusive treatments of scholarly questions, although the unfinished or inconclusive treatment may often be a more valuable contribution to its field, especially if it represents an intellectual impasse. Still further, the argument holds, some university publishers are far too prone to set themselves up as venturesome arbiters of scholarly taste, bringing enlightenment to backward areas of scholarship by means of planned publishing programs, when they are neither well equipped to know what scholarship needs nor sufficiently receptive to truly challenging manuscripts to justify their pretensions to leadership.

Once again we can hardly accept the criticism in the terms in which it is put, and indeed there is one forceful rebuttal to it in which scholars as well as other commentators join: the scholar who has not written a book but only gathered some materials together has not been sufficiently thoughtful about his subject and his materials to develop a bona fide contribution to scholarship, and under the circumstances he cannot expect to put someone else to the expense of publishing what he has written. But even though there are undoubtedly many instances in which scholarly authors should have thought more clearly about the problems they were dealing with, this argument is more nearly a restatement than a resolution of the central issue. Experienced scholars continue to wish for the dissemination of aesthetically unsatisfying results of research on the plausible supposition that unless such crude materials are published—and in conveniently usable form—the study that went into them is likely to be a dead loss to scholarship, which depends upon a gradual accumulation of data as well as an occasional intellectual break-through.

Furthermore, the critical part of the discussion focuses on the manuscript that cannot under any circumstances count upon a sale of more than a few hundred copies. Granted that few university presses can now afford to publish such works on their own initiative, the fact makes less rather than more reason why their criteria of publishability should be applied to *all* kinds of scholarly writing. Much important scholarship, especially in obscure or unpopular fields of study, is by definition esoteric, and any attempt to restate it in more generally accessible terms would often be a disservice to humane learning. It may be that only a "book" can sell effectively, or stir the sympathies of a scholarly publisher, but our criterion must ultimately be the needs and usages that scholars themselves define.

Several kinds of information gathered during the course of our inquiry cast light on this aspect of scholarly publishing and its problems. One is the fact that no matter how scrupulous the process of reviewing manuscripts may be—and no matter how completely the financial deliberations of a press's governing authority are isolated from the expert deliberations of its scholarly readers and editors—most presses attempt to publish most of their books for a relatively wide market. They have no choice; in the words of one press director, "If our market were restricted to scholars and libraries, we would go out of business in six weeks." But the inference is nonetheless unavoidable that the size of the market influences publishing judgment, and that the manuscript with small potential circulation must justify itself in ways that the manuscript with a larger potential circulation need not always provide.

One basis for such a contention is the actual figures on printings, sales, and other crucial phenomena of university publishing, which at first glance suggest a contrary view. For whereas twenty-seven presses that provided usable data reported first printings of over 1300 copies for 77 per cent of the unsubsidized books they published in a given year, they reported equally large printings for only 51 per cent of their subsidized titles.[2] Of the 49 per cent of subsidized books for which first printings ran to less than 1301 copies, moreover, almost half—22 per cent of the total—were printed in editions of less than 801. On this basis we might conclude both that a large number of books were published upon subsidy and that university presses were heavily committed to small-edition publishing.

Nevertheless, these figures must be understood in context. In the first place, several small printings involved works published simultaneously abroad, which means that the total number of

[2] Only twenty-two of the twenty-seven presses reported subsidized books. Here and in what follows a subsidized book is defined as one the publication of which made use of a specific fund or appropriation made available for the support of scholarly publication by a philanthropic foundation, a learned society, a university department, or an author. It excludes books published upon the general operating funds of a press even when those funds included financial support from a parent university.

copies printed was considerably higher than the American press figures indicate. Secondly, as many as 41 subsidized titles may have been published on the initiative of department or faculty committees, or at least without the exercise of complete editorial discretion by the presses involved.[3] Had one-half of these titles been published in press runs of less than 801, as presumably a large number of them were, and had they been subtracted from the subsidized totals reported, the proportion of small subsidized editions to total subsidized titles would have fallen from 22 per cent to 15 per cent. Hence while the corrected figures are not conclusive because of certain gaps and anomalies in the data we have, they nonetheless lend support to the contention that even in undertaking to publish books on a subsidy basis university presses frequently expect them to sell a relatively large number of copies.

It is true, of course, that first printings of subsidized works may deliberately be made large, because (as a few press directors commented) it is so much cheaper to produce five hundred extra copies in unbound sheets than to set up the machinery again for a second printing. Nevertheless, such sales figures as we have from a number of presses tend to reinforce our contention. In the final version of our questionnaire presses were asked to report the sales of subsidized titles during the first two years after their publication, or during another but roughly comparable period. Although we have usable data from only fifteen presses and figures for only 124 subsidized volumes out of a total of 172 they

[3] The figure is based upon an assumption that volumes reported as subsidized included all those published without complete editorial discretion.

Our figures on this point are inconclusive because we asked the presses to report only titles in series published without the exercise of complete discretion on their part. But if, as seems likely, nondiscretionary publication is numerically a function of the publication of substantially unrevised doctoral dissertations, we know that 16 titles in series (compared with 20 unrevised dissertations published in series) were published without discretion, and we may infer that an additional 25 titles not in series (16/20 of 31 unrevised dissertations published as independent titles) probably constituted nondiscretionary volumes, for a total of 41 such volumes among 495 published by twenty-seven presses.

In addition, two large presses published 76 volumes (of which 56 were substantially unrevised doctoral dissertations and 72 titles in series) without exercising complete editorial discretion, making a grand total of 117 such volumes out of a total of 604 reported by twenty-nine presses. Because of the unusual nature of their operations, however, these titles have not been incorporated into the totals used in the text.

reported, and although their replies provided information on sales during periods ranging from as little as seven months to as much as two years, it seems significant that 42 per cent of the reported titles had already sold over half of their first printings, whereas only 19 per cent had sold less than three-tenths. This is not to say that university presses normally expect to sell a great many copies of titles for which they require subventions, for 72 per cent of the titles reported had sold no more than eight hundred copies. But it does suggest that for the most part first printings of subsidized works are an accurate if not a conservative index of anticipated sales. This tends to confirm rather than to challenge the contention that a highly specialized manuscript often confronts a sales test that it finds difficulty in meeting successfully.

Finally, university presses seem to operate on a general premise that within certain limits it is necessary for them to break even (recover their own editorial and manufacturing costs) on a large number of subsidized titles. The data we have on this point are highly tentative, because the presses could only guess at many of the essential figures, but it seems clear both from the specific figures and from the general expressions of opinion we received in answer to our questions that most presses hope to recover their own costs on something like two-thirds of the books for which they receive subsidies.[4] Of course there is nothing to be surprised at in this attitude, which simply reflects the financial realities of contemporary publishing, but like so many other understandable facts it serves to lend strength to our belief that there is relatively little room in modern university publishing for the manuscript of clear scholarly merit that cannot count upon at least a modest public sale. Moreover, the fact that a concededly outstanding esoteric manuscript faces no such problem, whether or not it finally qualifies for a subsidy, is irrelevant here. Although, like a good commercial press, a university press is willing sometimes to invest its funds in prestigious publication that cannot possibly produce a profit, the obvious effect of making such investments in prestige is to reduce still further the financial possibility of publishing less distinguished but clearly valuable manuscripts. Neither the conditions of contemporary publishing nor the uni-

---

[4] By contrast they expect to break even on *the first printings* of only about 40 per cent of the unsubsidized volumes they reported.

versity presses' established ways of meeting them provide adequate ways of publishing good but not great manuscripts of small potential circulation.

Indeed it is fair to say that press directors more or less concede that some worthwhile manuscripts go unpublished because of extrinsic considerations. Sometimes they have been willing to say so outright, and to plead for some means of solving the problem without disadvantage either to scholars or to presses. More often they have reported that no worthy scholarly manuscript of normal size goes unpublished in the United States today but have made clear simultaneously that they were thinking of manuscripts that could count upon selling one thousand or more copies over a period of several years. Confronted with the proposition that a manuscript with a potential sale of no more than five or six hundred copies may therefore constitute a problem of publication, they have generally adopted one or another of three main positions: first, that the "social cost" of disseminating the esoteric results of specialized research by normal publishing means far outweighs the social advantages of publication; second, that the esoteric work promising only a slight sale is by definition not a truly valuable contribution to scholarship; and third, that some means should be found to make such products available inexpensively, as through micropublication and direct-mail distribution to interested scholars.

We shall consider the utility of microreproduction in solving problems of scholarly publication later in this report. What is significant here is that while each of these separate reactions is plausible by itself, all three taken together have the effect of confirming rather than denying the existence of genuine problems of publication. The first is convincing until the second makes clear that social cost is likely to be confused with the quality of research, while the third casts doubt on both the first and the second by implying that some kinds of esoteric publications should take place but cannot under present arrangements. Hence the real burden of the presses' argument is that *they* should not be held responsible for the publication of certain kinds of scholarly manuscripts—not that no means of publication should be found for them—and few press spokesmen seem to feel that the problem of the esoteric manuscript is on the way to solution, except perhaps for those who have become impatient with continued agitation of the subject.

Nevertheless, the candid observer must acknowledge that a sizable part of the clamor for the publication of uneconomic scholarly manuscripts reflects a wish to see into print a substantial percentage of doctoral dissertations, and it is clear that some of this clamor is not really evidence of a problem of scholarly publication. For one thing, experienced scholars, as well as unsuccessful authors, often make use of essentially tangential arguments for publication of the doctoral thesis: it is a necessary impetus to a man's career as a scholar; it is an important means of maintaining the scholarly standards and standing of a great university; it educates the novice writer by putting him in touch with leading scholars in his field. Yet no advocate of thesis publication proposes that every dissertation be published (although some insist that every dissertation should be publishable), so that a question of selection inevitably arises in any discussion of the problem. Perhaps the most plausible way of stating the scholars' case, therefore, would be to argue that the thesis should not be discriminated against *as* a thesis, but that neither should it be considered a special category of publication.

At the same time, to the extent that the manuscript with small potential sale is dissociated from the thesis it takes on greater significance, for it reflects the expressed needs of experienced scholars as scholars rather than as authors or teachers. According to them, the scholarly monograph and the monograph series published either by a university or by a learned society are important tools of further scholarly inquiry, which incidentally make room for occasional valuable dissertations that would otherwise be buried. These monograph series are particularly important, moreover, in areas of scholarship such as Classics and Linguistics and kinds of scholarship such as field reports in Anthropology and Folklore that could not under any circumstances attract a wide public. Indeed, the utility of monograph series in such fields is already widely agreed to, and what is truly at issue is whether in order to see publication an author or a field worker should be required to provide part or all of the funds necessary for printing his work. But this is part of the larger problem of author subsidies, which affects every area of scholarly endeavor to a greater or lesser extent, and which is best discussed in general rather than in specific terms.

In general, directors of university presses and scholars are more nearly in agreement on the issue of author subsidies than on the scholarly merits of the manuscripts that most often create the pressure for subventions. That is, there is a widespread sentiment, in which both parties share, that no scholar should be asked except in extraordinary cases to subsidize his own manuscript. The case has not always stood thus, and individuals may still be found to urge that a scholar can well afford to contribute toward the costs of his publication because he receives a generous financial return from the promotions and salary raises that ensue. Furthermore, it is argued that the scholar is far better off financially than the author of *belles lettres*, for in a lifetime he makes far more money from his scholarship and teaching together than even the author of an ordinary best-seller. Yet few scholars and still fewer directors of university presses seem to feel that these commercial arguments carry much conviction. On one hand they point out that the average scholar today can hardly afford to divert a large part of one year's income even temporarily, and they insist that any attempt to calculate his financial returns must also recognize both the large investment he puts into his education and the large investment he puts into research long before he can think of starting to write, not to mention the fact that he seldom if ever recovers his total investment in cash as a popular author can.

On the other hand the rebuttal also runs, even more powerfully, that publication of a scholarly manuscript should in every case depend upon a reasoned judgment of its utility to scholarship, and an author's private wealth or his willingness to mortgage his future should not determine what is published in a country as rich as ours. There is, indeed, a kind of middle ground occupied by the doctoral dissertation, which leads some scholars at institutions in which authors are still asked to contribute as much as half of the cost of publication of their theses to suggest that the best they can hope for is a limit on the amount an author may provide. But it seems legitimate to suppose that this middle ground exists only because in such institutions publication of the doctoral dissertation is expected if not required; and surely it would be preferable to hold all publishing and all manuscripts to a single standard of scholarship, rather than treat an unhappy compromise as a basis for future policy-making. So, at least, most scholars and most press directors seem to feel.

Hence we cannot legitimately solve the problem of short-press-run manuscripts either by denying their utility to scholars, as some press statements seem to imply, or by exhorting scholars to invest in their own futures, as a number of them apparently have. If press and scholarly activities continue to follow precedent there will continue to be problems of scholarly publication, which will worsen as the costs of publishing rise. The question, then, becomes one of what to do, rather than whether to take action.

Those who are skeptical of the problems scholars describe tend to recommend almost automatically that they seek some form of micropublication (microfilm, Microcards, Microprint) for the works university presses cannot handle. Certainly if micropublication were an effective and useful means of disseminating the results of research, the prejudices that some scholars obviously hold against it would carry little weight and the problem of publishing esoteric manuscripts would virtually disappear. But although there are appropriate uses for microforms in scholarly publishing, and although scholars and administrators are probably insufficiently ready to accept them on their merits, it is clear that micropublication cannot solve the problems we have described.

There are a number of powerful reasons. In the first place, each form of micropublication suffers from characteristic mechanical defects. Each creates eyestrain, each is excessively subject to wear, each defies easy handling and contemplative reading or re-reading, each precludes useful marginal notes and memoranda. Moreover, each requires a special reading device that is both cumbersome and disproportionately expensive, yet each also presents characteristic advantages for retrieving certain kinds of fugitive material, so that short of a technological breakthrough there is little likelihood that we shall have a single standard microform and an appropriately convenient and inexpensive reading machine within the reach of every scholar. This is not to say that no scholarly publication should ever be relegated to microforms—Microcards are especially appropriate for disseminating auxiliary matter employed in current research, such as extensive tabulations in Economics, just as microfilm is appropriate for making copies of old documents available to scattered historians—but it is clear that a completed report on scholarly research can hardly be considered to have been published when it has been reproduced in this fashion.

Perhaps the most promising recent development associated with micropublication, therefore, has been the XeroX process employed by University Microfilms, Inc., for the more convenient dissemination of materials already available on microfilm.[5] By this means the microfilmed pages of a scholarly manuscript are transferred electrostatically to a continuous sheet of ordinary paper, which is then folded and bound loosely together to form what amounts to a book in the traditional sense. Given the existence of microfilmed copy the process of reproduction is relatively inexpensive, and with further technical advances it may soon make possible the offset printing of works for which a very small sale is anticipated at considerably less expense than they now require.

But though from a mechanical point of view the XeroX process avoids most of the difficulties inherent in microform publication, it has in common with microforms the difficulty of establishing adequate editorial control over what is published. When employed, as at present, to reproduce doctoral dissertations and out-of-print books, Xerography draws upon the expert editorial assistance of the university faculty who accepted a dissertation or the editors and scholarly referees who recommended a book. Were it to be applied to the original publication of manuscripts other than doctoral dissertations, however, there would be no way of exercising control over what was published save by introducing many of the editorial functions and consequently the editorial overhead that already creates difficulties for university presses. Without such provisions, on the other hand, it would be likely to result in the publication of inferior volumes of scholarship, and hence to discredit auxiliary publication in book form for good as well as bad reasons.

Nor is the credit in which such publication is held an un-

[5] The same process, a property of Haloid-XeroX Inc., may also be applied to the single-copy reproduction of any book that is out of print, at a cost of three and one-half cents per page plus binding, provided a usable copy is available.

important matter. Although bad books continue to be published under editorial supervision, and although any scholar insists upon making his own judgments of the works that he reads, a title available only in unfamiliar form automatically confronts far graver obstacles in gaining recognition and circulation according to its merits than does the ordinary university press book. It is more than likely that a considerable body of auxiliary publications would not be reviewed and might not even be listed in most scholarly journals, and no publishers' catalogue could be devised that would serve the purposes of a buyer who wished to acquire titles selectively. It is true that he could order every title apparently reflecting his field of professional interest, but it seems unrealistic to suppose that he would, and no more realistic to think that he should. Without the regular exercise of editorial discretion before printing, and without critical examination of what has been printed, that is, true publication cannot take place, and unless some means can be found to combine the technical advantages of the XeroX process with at least a minimum of scholarly editing the promise it holds out for facilitating scholarly publication will not be realized.

Putting the matter in this way, however, also serves to remind us that the physical appearance of a publication need have no relevance to its utility or even to its reception, and that unjustified typewriter composition (whether printed by offset or by Xerography) is often a legitimate means of solving contemporary problems of scholarly publication. Of course certain kinds of scholarly material will not reproduce adequately by direct photographic means, and in some cases it may be more economical to set type on a monotype machine than to make clean typewriter copy and convert it to photographic plates. So-called near-print techniques are no panacea, and indeed most university presses report that they know when and how to use substitutes for letterpress, and when a manuscript or its potential audience will not permit them. But although many publishers report that they already use near-print when they wish to, many of them would also welcome a more tolerant attitude toward it on the part of scholars in the humanities, who have been too inclined to confuse the mechanics with the merits of a publication. Nevertheless, there seems to be little likelihood that typewriter composition offers a permanent solution to the problems of scholarly publication, for it grows more expensive as unionization raises the wages of typist-compositors, and it presents characteristic technical difficulties.[6]

Hence the problem of the esoteric manuscript, like the other problems that have been discussed during the course of this account of scholarly publishing, is amenable only to a judicious use of additional funds; it is not to be "solved" by being relegated to a form of publication markedly inferior to what learned societies and universities and university presses already provide. As such it becomes one with other problems of publication that have already been discussed and which we may pass in review here by way of suggesting the most plausible kinds of assistance for scholarly book publication in the United States.

In the first place, of course, there are a number of problems that can be effectively solved only by special appropriations of

[6] This is an appropriate place to comment on the suggestion, made frequently by scholars, that the university presses economize in the publication of scholarly volumes by binding them in paper covers. Some volumes are in fact paper-bound, especially those for which only a small general sale is anticipated; probably, therefore, the scholars' recommendation has relevance chiefly for the categories of publication in which there does not seem to be a pressing problem, although it is possible that university press sales might increase if press books were more often available in both bindings. (Twenty-nine presses that responded to our questionnaire reported publishing 571 books, of which 483, or 85 per cent, appeared exclusively in hard covers, as compared with 67 in paper covers and 21 in both.) On the other hand the presses are understandably reluctant to bind in paper covers even esoteric works for which a continued use is anticipated because university libraries—which are one of the main markets for these titles—are then put to the expensive task of binding each of them individually. Furthermore, there is some question whether most of the scholars who recommend paper bindings fully understand the economics of publishing. Paper-bound reprints make money in press runs of 10,000 or 20,000 copies, but few original scholarly titles could be expected to sell that many copies in any form whatsoever, and the individual purchaser of a scholarly book that appeared in a small press run would not save much by virtue of a paper cover alone.

Scholars might be better advised to question the policy of university presses with respect to discounts. Twenty presses that published 192 subsidized books reported offering 37 per cent of these titles for sale at exclusively trade discounts, and an additional 8 per cent at some combination of trade and text discounts. To the extent that scholarly titles can reach a wide audience through commercial bookstores the trade discount is essential, but one wonders whether all of these subsidized titles were expected to reach that larger audience. If not, their sale price was considerably higher than it need have been, and the small discount some scholars may have received on direct-mail sales did not compensate for the exaggerated list price.

some sort. These include most of the categories on which press directors and scholars almost uniformly agree—works requiring expensive composition, or constituting tools of effective scholarship, or extending to many volumes. ("Short books," while they are also universally acknowledged to be a problem, are less amenable to the mere provision of additional funds, and will be dealt with in Chapter 4.) Nor does the administration of funds offer as many difficulties in this area as in some others. Although a majority of press directors would probably prefer to make their own use of funds awarded, like the Ford grants, on an undifferentiated basis, it would seem that special awards in aid of extraordinary costs of publication administered by some scholarly body would be acceptable to them. While many expressed hostility to any system of special awards, primarily on the grounds that it introduces inelasticity and uncertainties and delays into a publishing venture that is already hard put to be effective because of the multiplicity of interests it serves, their objections applied with particular force to manuscripts of ordinary size and qualities competing for a place in a publishing program. The chief characteristic of the manuscripts we are discussing here, however, is that they make such disproportionate obstacles to publication as to require distinctive treatment apart from the "ordinary" activities of the presses. Presumably, therefore, they should be supported by special awards according to need rather than by general appropriations among a number of presses.

Manuscripts of esoteric works that are not dictionaries nor bibliographies nor compilations present a somewhat different kind of problem. In general, university presses prefer not to handle many of them if they can avoid doing so, and there is some question as to whether either general appropriations or special awards would significantly increase their commitment to this form of publishing. Yet some means must be found among the devices for effective publication available to us: one likely vehicle is the monograph series. When sponsored by a learned society it has the advantage of acknowledged scholarly criteria and a ready-made scholarly audience, and at the same time it avoids the drawbacks of departmentally controlled publication—not only the informal pressures that various commentators hint at, but also the exclusiveness that most institutional series entail. Furthermore, it is the spokesmen for learned societies rather than scholars at large who have most strenuously called our attention to the problem of the esoteric manuscript, and apparently a number of them have already had experience in the publication of such manuscripts. (Indeed several of them have protested that while a monograph series is an excellent device for publishing esoteric matter, the monograph principle has been undermined by the extent to which lack of funds has forced editors of monograph series to publish what authors are willing to subsidize rather than select rigorously among submitted manuscripts.) Finally, of course, if scholars protest that university presses do not or cannot make publishing decisions solely in terms of scholarly needs, what more plausible device is there for rectifying this situation than that of making possible publication under the auspices of the appropriate learned society?

Nevertheless, objections do arise. For one thing, some scholarly authors in the humanities seem almost as reluctant to publish under such auspices as to commit their works to near-print. Except insofar as college and university administrators might fail to honor learned-society publication, however, this hardly seems a compelling objection, and it is wholly unimportant in the more esoteric fields in which the problems of small-circulation manuscripts are most acute. A second and more plausible objection is that the officers and leading members of learned societies cannot easily find time to administer a selective program of publication sponsored by the society. This is a point on which we have accumulated no scholarly observations or reflections, but it seems to suggest rather that grants in aid of esoteric publication take into account the need for honoraria than that they not be made at all; and of course there is nothing in any potential awards system that forces the officers of a learned society to seek funds they do not wish to administer. For that matter, it might be preferable to ask learned societies merely to recommend certain manuscripts, which would be judged in the final analysis by joint councils or committees of learned societies rather than by the individual bodies.

Finally, some mention should also be made of the fact that special awards might threaten to create a degree of harmful competition between learned societies and university presses—harmful to the extent that learned societies attempted to publish profitable books that would achieve equal or greater circulation by other means. In the nature of the case the danger seems slight (scholars do not usually approach learned societies before they have tried their manuscripts on university presses, or university presses before they have sounded out at least one trade publisher), but perhaps a condition might be imposed in assigning awards that would prevent the use of monograph funds in support of prize publication such as the American Historical Association and the Modern Language Association engage in. There are good scholarly reasons for initiating prize competitions, but few of them are connected with the problems of publication we have been discussing.[7]

In sum, then, there is need for a large general fund that may be awarded, upon application by learned societies, for the publication of monographs or monograph series within their respective fields. Certainly the likeliest alternative vehicle for such publications, the university monograph series sponsored by the faculty of a particular department or college, seems a far less attractive means for solving the problems that obviously exist. Questions of doubtful criteria and institutional exclusiveness aside, a single national society makes a far more effective means of administering funds in aid of publication in a particular field than a small handful of university departments that normally publish only a few monographs a year. A society must have adequate funds if it is not to be faced with the necessity for discriminating among manuscripts for financial rather than scholarly reasons, but it is clearly more capable of developing a coherent publishing program. Of course neither system will make room for the distinctive manuscript that falls outside the scope of any single discipline, and here the objections that scholars as authors and scholars as users of books make to scholars as university press referees have particular relevance; but perhaps it is legitimate to suggest that if scholars can find a way to publish the kinds of study that are already accepted, the university presses will be somewhat freer

[7] The most pertinent reason is the wish to encourage good writing among scholars in a field; others include a wish to stimulate study in certain areas, a wish to establish standards of intellectual performance, even a wish to improve scholarly morale. None, it will be noted, involves an assumption that publication itself is difficult.

to ignore established scholarly boundaries in their own publishing programs. Certainly the possibility should be congenial to their hopes.

What has been said puts the financial burden of solving contemporary problems in book publication upon whatever philanthropic agencies are willing to provide necessary funds, while it makes the administration of such funds a concern of the learned societies or their councils. Nevertheless, American colleges and universities can also contribute significantly to the solution of current needs. Obviously some already sponsor publication under a university press imprint; a handful of others have working arrangements with a variety of publishers that facilitate publication by members of their faculties through what amounts to a privately administered system of awards in aid of publication, or make such awards on an *ad hoc* basis; but a large number neither sponsor nor facilitate publication even of worthwhile manuscripts, acting on the theory that publication should be a matter of competitive success and ignoring the extent to which circumstances may make it difficult. Their attitude and their practice may well be considered to aggravate existing problems, which they might better undertake to deal with constructively.

Presumably it would not be wise for additional universities to set up their own presses, at least not until the fate and publishing effectiveness of a number of recently established presses are more clearly decided. Quite probably they should also hesitate to encourage faculty-initiated publication, both because of the suspicions it creates and because of the exclusiveness it entails. But there seems to be no good nonfinancial reason why institutions that make no contribution to scholarly publishing today should not contribute to the cost of publishing one of their own scholars' manuscripts when it has been accepted by a qualified university press and when the only obstacle to its publication is a shortage of funds. Certainly such a program in aid of publication would seem to be especially appropriate to those in which there is any semblance of a "publication requirement" for the faculty; and a nationwide policy under which every college and university awarded grants in aid of publication with bona fide university presses on a regular basis should do much to remove the last difficulties that still interfere with effective dissemination of the results of scholarly research—and without adding noticeably to the financial burdens of the average college or small university.

Finally, scholars themselves can contribute something toward the solution of contemporary publishing problems by presenting university and other publishers with more nearly adequate manuscripts. There is probably little they can do on their own initiative to write the better books that some commentators insist would make scholarly publishing simple—and this is a comment on observers who seek to define away the problem of publication by holding scholarly authors to standards they have never before observed in the United States. But there is no reason why they cannot prepare manuscripts that are legible, literate, and well-organized. Some publishers recommend that scholars hire professionally trained typists to prepare the final drafts of their manuscripts, but others suggest that suitable typists are not always accessible, and presumably many scholars might have difficulty in paying their fees if they were. Perhaps partly for this reason, several press directors expressed a wish that graduate schools would give greater attention to training potential authors in their literary and mechanical responsibilities, but one or two of them more or less admitted that this sort of education is unlikely to receive a high priority or even an effective place in graduate training, which is already crowded with requirements; and of course it is hardly a solution to today's problems to educate another generation of scholars. For such reasons the learned societies might wish to consider sponsoring, as an outgrowth of this inquiry, a brief pamphlet of instructions and recommendations to scholarly authors. It can hardly be argued that such instructions are not already plentifully available, but perhaps a sponsored précis of current advice and information would help to teach authors how to behave and what to expect in publishing.

Any gains that were made, the reports of the press directors imply, would tend to diminish the time-consuming chores of publishing and thus to leave university presses freer for creative publishing activities. This should in fact be the over-all effect of any programs in aid of scholarly publishing that the learned societies undertake to sponsor. Here and there the proposed innovations might lead to more paperwork and additional conferences, but for the most part the easing of contemporary difficulties should increase the scope and flexibility of the publishing that is now going on. Of course no program of aid can insure perfection, and certainly the delays and the controversies that occasionally afflict the consideration and the publication of scholarly manuscripts today will continue to occur, but were all the recommendations this report embraces effectively carried out it is difficult to see what problems of book publication would continue to be critical.

4.

The Publication of Scholarly Journals

Like the directors of university presses, editors of seventy-five leading journals in the humanities and social sciences were asked to fill out an elaborate questionnaire covering the number of manuscripts submitted and accepted or rejected during the course of a year, the editorial procedures and criteria employed in the review process, the economics and other technical aspects of publication, and additional matters of judgment and perspective that only experienced editors could comment on. Like the press questionnaire this demanded a considerable amount of work on the part of everyone who answered it, but sixty-seven editors replied, almost all of them in detail. Meanwhile we supplemented the questionnaire with personal interviews wherever they were possible, which brought the total number of journals from which we have information to seventy-two.[1]

The evidence that we gathered by these means indicates that in general the problems affecting publication in learned journals are less acute than the problems of scholarly book publication in the United States. This is presumably an inevitable and even a logical situation, because under present circumstances most scholarly books must appeal to an audience somewhat larger than the body of professional scholars for whom an author may in the first instance have written, whereas the reverse is often true of journal publication. Many journals are published for only a few actual subscribers besides the university libraries that habitually buy publications in almost every field of scholarship, and although they perform a number of valuable scholarly functions they may often be more important as outlets for work in progress than as repositories of completed scholarship.

[1] The journals on which the statements in this chapter are based are listed in Appendix E.

Nevertheless this statement of the journals' function conceals a significant paradox. Unless they are organs of learned societies attracting large memberships for other reasons, few scholarly journals can pay their own way even as successfully as the average scholarly book, and hence in purely arithmetical terms they are probably worse off financially than most university presses. What dissolves the paradox is the common practice (and the common assumption) that a journal will find means of supporting itself without large subscription lists and without extensive direct subsidies. The means employed are worth brief consideration here before we turn to a discussion of problems that arise within the established practice of journal publication.

In the first place it is probably accurate to say that scholars themselves contribute as much as anyone to the publication of learned journals. Presumably it is unimportant that an author can almost never expect to receive even token sums in payment for his articles, and perhaps it can be held that a scholar reviewing a new book is sufficiently compensated for his time and skills by the appearance of his review and by the expansion of his professional library, but these are nevertheless evidences of an unpaid scholarly contribution to the economics of journal publication. Moreover, a far more significant contribution comes in the form of the editorial services and functions that any journal provides and that are almost never adequately reimbursed. For one thing, while most editors of scholarly journals receive honoraria or partial relief from teaching duties or both, they perform most of their labors on time that other scholars can consider "free" and for sums that are hardly commensurate with their obligations—and they have even been known to refuse compensation on the grounds that their journals need the money more. Still further, they depend in turn upon the voluntary labors of a whole corps of distinguished scholars who read submitted manuscripts and make editorial recommendations about them. The distinction between book and article publication is in fact nicely illustrated here, for the same scholar who may be invited to act as an underpaid scholarly referee for a university press may also serve as a wholly unpaid referee for a learned journal. Without such labors journal publication would be virtually impossible.

Still other agencies also contribute significantly to the publication of learned journals. If scholars donate time to editorial services, it is only because their colleges and universities permit them to do so, at what is inevitably some cost to the effective pursuit of their other responsibilities—not merely teaching and administration, but also in many cases scholarship itself. The fact that such institutions may hope to recover their outlay in the form of academic prestige hardly alters the magnitude of their contribution, especially when allowance is also made for the hidden subsidies that almost all journals cost their sponsors. Our inquiry has shown that journals generally make use of college and university office and storage space, utilities, and sometimes even mailing facilities at far less than their actual cost; that they draw upon institutional funds not only to pay the salaries of editors but also to provide for innumerable secretarial and staff costs and services; that they often receive some form of subsidy—direct or indirect —from the university presses that handle the printing and distribution of many of them; and that in emergencies they may receive still further financial assistance. Certainly journal publication—unlike much university press publication—would cease in all but a handful of cases were institutional sponsorship to come to a halt; and few even of the nominally self-sufficient journals could continue publication without the sponsorship of their parent societies.

The point of these remarks is not to exaggerate the obstacles that journals face but to place their current problems in context. On one hand the fact that many of them confront recurring difficulties in meeting publication costs should not be considered prima facie evidence of a serious emergency in scholarly publishing; shortages of funds seem to be endemic. But it is at least equally true that when they confront rapidly rising costs of production they have almost nowhere to turn for assistance. Increased circulation is probably nearly impossible for any but the already prosperous publications; increased subscription rates, especially if they are to match increased costs, are probably equally implausible in a great many cases; cheaper techniques of production such as typewriter composition with unjustified margins might well alienate a sufficient number of nonlibrary subscribers as to destroy the advantages gained through such economies—if, indeed, they would be economies in all instances. In any event, confronted with rising costs, scholar-editors have usually preferred to reduce the size of their publications by turning away or skeletonizing publishable articles, by excluding supporting matter that has traditionally accompanied scholarly essays, and by neglecting areas of scholarly interest such as review articles and annotated bibliographies that might well be considered essential services to scholarship today. Quite possibly—as some editors have observed—the shrinking process has had beneficial side effects on contemporary scholarly writing, but to the extent that the shrinkage has arisen because of financial pressures it suggests a problem worth more extended consideration.

By all odds the gravest problem of publication that editors of scholarly journals report is the manuscript that is too long for an article yet too short for a book. Some few journals accept articles of fifty or sixty printed pages or even more, and a few are organs of learned societies that publish monograph series in which manuscripts too long for the journal may be printed, but the great majority of publications simply cannot devote so many pages to a single essay, and even the journal that publishes one long essay is thereby precluded from publishing another immediately afterward. Nor does serializing a long study help matters much, for although it spreads out the burden of printing so many pages it does not increase the amount of space available to the journal, and it may do a disservice to the essay that is divided. (Certainly it does a disservice to the reader who wishes to make use of an essay in its entirety.) Moreover, a number of editors suggest that if it were possible for them to continue to meet their other publishing obligations meanwhile they would welcome opportunities to print not only extended essays but also other kinds of scholarly material (documents, translations, special bibliographies) that are now generally excluded from publication by virtue of their awkward size. Clearly there is ample evidence here that space is needed for manuscripts of intermediate size, and the problem is to find ways of publishing them without encroaching on the other functions of the learned journals.

For that matter any long manuscript, even when it is too short to be considered as an independent publication, causes many journals extraordinary difficulties, for the usual limit on the length an article may run is twenty-five printed pages, and it is sometimes considerably less. Again the problem is one of space, but there is an important difference in its implications. Presumably most essays and other independent titles of seventy-five or one hundred printed pages might and indeed should be published separately if some economical means could be found to accomplish the task. In all probability, however, shorter essays should be incorporated into the pages of an appropriate journal, not only because journal publication would be more efficient, but also because it would be foolish to multiply the vehicles of publication when existing journals wish to find ways of increasing their own publishing scope. Here the nature of the problem points to a simple and indeed almost mechanical solution: additional funds would make possible printing of additional pages when suitable manuscripts were on hand.

In a sense the problem of space that the journals complain of parallels the problem of the multivolume work that the university presses report, in that difficulties arise when an editor tries to expand his publication; and of course the need for a vehicle for manuscripts of intermediate size is also directly attested to by the press directors. It can hardly be surprising, therefore, that other problems the university presses reported also find a parallel in our poll of editors of scholarly journals.

The most pressing seems to be the difficulty of printing suitable illustrations and other matter to accompany studies in such fields of scholarship as Art History, Musicology, Archaeology, and Medieval Studies, and the analogous difficulty of paying for unusually difficult composition in such varied fields as Linguistics, Economics, Romance Languages, and Sociology, and in such different forms as numerical tables, bibliography, and foreign languages. Although some of these problems (such as supporting tables in the social sciences and in Linguistics) may be amenable to near-print and even nonprint means of publication, which editors are admittedly reluctant to employ, it is becoming more and more common for scholarly journals in a number of fields to ask authors to contribute part or all of the cost of illustration and special composition, and failing that to exclude or to reduce the scope of such materials if not to refuse an article entirely. Tables are eliminated, articles in foreign languages are translated, bibliographical aids are abandoned, illustrations are reduced in number and quality. Moreover while it is true that in many fields of scholarship an author's contribution to the cost of printing any single article will probably be small, obviously the costs of composition of a number of articles in hard-pressed fields will mount up, and such costs *begin* high in those calling for faithful representation of works of art. In some journals, of course—the *Art Bulletin* is one—authors are not permitted to contribute to the costs of illustration, but the effect of this scruple is simply to increase the annual deficit that a journal must make up from voluntary contributions—a deficit that has recently led the *Art Bulletin* to abandon collotype for offset printing in spite of the latter's shortcomings. There is a distinct problem of publication here, even if in all probability its dimensions are smaller than those of the corresponding problem scholarly book publishers face.

In addition there is some reason to believe that individual scholarly journals are harder pressed today than their intrinsic merits warrant—that, in other words, they have been or may be forced to curtail publication for economic rather than scholarly reasons, and for lack of general funds rather than lack of funds for special purposes. Even if some form of support is found for the extraordinary costs of publishing work in Art History and Criticism, for example, scholarship there will continue to suffer from the disappearance of the *Magazine of Art*, and the *Art Bulletin* may be expected to face mounting financial difficulties. Much the same thing is true of journals representing other fields of scholarship in which available financial resources simply do not match the demands that are made upon them, and in which every issue of the journal constitutes a personal triumph for the editor over mounting costs. Moreover, some journals have special reason to worry, not because they are without funds, but because they represent growing fields of scholarship, in which the number and variety of trained authors is advancing more rapidly than the vehicles for their work can be expected to expand. It is clear that there already are and that there will continue to be obstacles to the effective publication of scholarly articles in particular fields of contemporary scholarship, which the journals may not be able to solve by their own devices.

Finally, a number of editors, chiefly of journals in Literature, report that although they are satisfied that they can afford to print

54

what they wish to, publication may be delayed two years or more by the heavy backlog of acceptances to which they have committed themselves. Apparently one or two editors, nerved to the task by their pressing situation, have gone so far as to refuse all but an infinitesimal number of otherwise publishable articles until the current backlog is reduced to manageable proportions; but others who have been unwilling to turn away manuscripts on such extrinsic grounds plead for assistance in printing what they have already accepted, at least to the point at which the delay between acceptance and publication is no more than approximately one year.[2] Again the problem may be relatively insignificant, but presumably it would be a simple matter to cure by making available frankly emergency funds, upon suitable application, to enable a journal confronted with a backlog in excess of fifteen or eighteen months to print extra signatures and so catch up with its editorial acceptances.

But the question is not simply one of providing technically adequate and suitable large "outlets" for what scholars have written or may be expected to write within the foreseeable future. If university press directors wish for freedom to engage in more creative publishing and editing, so do editors of a number of distinguished learned journals—not only those incorporating research produced in expanding or interdisciplinary fields of scholarship, which offer the most immediate challenge to editorial leadership, but also those representing time-honored fields like History. Probably few scholarly editors who are also college or university professors could afford to devote additional hours to more energetic editing, but this in itself is a problem of scholarly publishing, and in any event there are editors who feel they could find the time if they were freed of some of their present mechanical obligations. Partly for this reason, it seems, a number of editors criticized their contributors for the drastic shortcomings of their manuscripts; and a few urged means to encourage better writing, whether through enlarged publishing initiative, or more extensive editorial correspondence with authors, or even token

[2] In most areas, at least in the humanities, a shorter period of delay is undesirable because it may force an editor to accept less than wholly satisfactory articles or drafts of articles rather than run the risk of having nothing to send to the printer; and of course great rapidity of publication is seldom critically important here as it is, by contrast, in the natural sciences.

payments for contributors. Obviously it is difficult to make a case for a problem of publication here if one considers scholarly journals as no more than so many available vehicles for scholarship, but clearly some experienced editors could use additional editorial resources, and quite possibly an expansion of editorial facilities would help improve the scholarly writing that book publishers as well as journal editors complain about.[3]

There is, moreover, a problem of expansion and diversification which confronts several journals that report no great pressure of surplus manuscripts, as well as some that sense great pressure. Editors representing a number of different fields of scholarship reported, for instance, that they cannot now accommodate review articles, which they hold to be as important to scholarship as the other services their journals offer, but which they cannot print to the exclusion either of substantive articles or of shorter notices of new books that must also be provided for their readers. Other editors particularly wish to enlarge either the number or the size of the reviews they carry, arguing that the short review, which has become more and more common as costs have risen, is virtually useless, and that an incomplete coverage of new books deprives a journal of one of its main reasons for existence. Still other editors seem relatively satisfied with the reviews their journals carry but would like to find room for other scholarly tools, especially bibliographies and finding lists but also in some cases documents and translations, that offer special difficulties under the present arrangements for journal publication. Without ruling on the merits of any of the particular instances the editors cite it is clear that they point to an area of publication that is peculiarly the province of the learned journals, and their wish to accomplish more is powerful evidence that a problem of scholarly publication exists.[4]

[3] We asked each of the editors whom we approached whether changes in the bad habits of scholarly authors would make any difference to either the volume or the rapidity of publication in their journals. By common consensus it would not. Some editors felt that they might be able to process manuscripts faster, but a great majority pointed out that their deliberate policy of maintaining a backlog of from two to four issues would prevent more rapid publication of accepted manuscripts, and almost all suggested that in any case the volume of publication is dependent exclusively upon the number of pages a journal can afford to print.
[4] Our inquiry has also suggested the existence of another kind of problem, closely related to what is described here although not formally within

Yet despite the existence of identifiable problems within the area of journal publication, attested to by editors and scholars alike, the evidence we have accumulated does not support unequivocally an argument that there is a widespread problem of scholarly publication in the learned journals. Some skeptics were willing to say, at least in private, that contemporary journals publish a great deal of "junk," while very few scholars whom we interviewed seemed to insist that significant problems of journal publication exist in the fields of study they know best. At the same time their views were often echoed by scholarly editors, who sometimes pointed out particular obstacles to publication that additional funds might solve, but who also held that there cannot be a problem of publication when so many vehicles are available for the manuscript any one journal turns down.

Oddly enough, however, these commonly expressed opinions may themselves constitute evidence of some kinds of publication problem, because the manifest content of such statements often seemed overshadowed by the circumstances in which they were made. So far as practicing scholars are concerned, for instance, many displayed an indifference to much of what is published in their fields of specialization that often seemed to reflect rather an exaggerated trust in what they themselves were doing than an objective evaluation of the many kinds of research that contribute to effective scholarship; and of course the assertion that "junk" is sometimes published does not justify an inference that nothing but junk goes unpublished. Significantly, no field of scholarship and no learned journal, however distinguished, seemed to escape entirely from such intemperate criticism. By the same token the editors' responses to our questions concerning submissions and acceptances of article manuscripts suggest that we should be cautious in assuming that where there are no complaints there is no problem. It is clear from their data, for example, that while many reputable journals accept approximately one-third or even one-

the scope of scholarly publication. This is the difficulty of publishing abstracts of current scholarly writing—a difficulty that threatens the future of such periodicals as *Historical Abstracts* and prevents the very existence of abstracts for other fields of scholarship. A large part of the problem, of course, is the expense of obtaining suitable abstracts; but the fact hardly denies that a problem exists for scholars.

half of the manuscripts submitted to them, leading journals in several fields of scholarship, especially Literature and History, accept as few as 15 per cent or even 10 per cent. Probably not much importance is to be attached to the fact by itself—it would not do to have them monopolize the good work in the field, and by virtue of their prestige they almost invariably attract first submissions of manuscripts that are more appropriate to less well-known publications—but it is important that their editors often seem to dismiss as of minor importance the question of what happens to the manuscripts that they turn away, and that editors of lesser journals also share in their indifference.

For that matter, the replies to two direct questions in our journals questionnaire were often quite revealing. Asked to tell us (1) How many manuscripts "meet your journal's normal standards for publication (irrespective, that is, of obstacles to publication such as special costs, considerations of space, or your wish to strike a balance in the contents)?" and (2) "How many of the manuscripts that meet your standards are you actually able to accept for publication?" a number of editors answered by treating the two questions as one, or otherwise clearly identified a manuscript's publishability with its acceptance. The very evidence that editors present, that is, implies that standards may vary with the immediate circumstances in which a journal finds itself, while the wish that editors of distinguished journals express, to publish the very best articles they can lay their hands on, may also militate against their ability to discern a problem where one exists.

Nevertheless, it is also important that the questionnaires we circulated among 2200 faculty members produced no direct evidence of problems in journal publication. The same reservations as to accuracy and relevance affect our use of the scholars' replies to questions about article manuscripts as affected our use of their data on book publication, especially because of the discrepancies between the rates of acceptance they reported and the rates estimated by editors of various journals, but certainly it would seem unwise to disregard the questionnaires entirely. In the six fields of scholarship for which we know the fate of more than fifty articles, for example (English and American Literature, American History, European History, Political Science, Philosophy, and

French), only in English and American Literature, with 77 per cent of 243 manuscripts accepted, does the rate of acceptance reported by scholars fall below 81 per cent, and in none of the smaller fields is it less than 95 per cent.[5] Indeed to the extent that we are able to reconcile these figures with the especially low rates of acceptance reported by prominent journals in European History (17 per cent), Literature (20 per cent), Philosophy (23 per cent), and American History (24 per cent), as by eliminating an undefined proportion of unscholarly submissions, by noting the extent to which unsurveyed journals may publish studies that major journals will not accept, by assuming on the basis of the scholars' replies to our question about unsuccessful manuscripts that the average article is submitted to more than one journal, and by attributing some discrepancies to exaggerated estimates of annual submissions, there is little reason to believe that genuine problems exist apart from those the editors themselves describe.

On the other hand it seems probable that unsuccessful authors were less likely, for a number of different reasons, to make out a full list of article manuscripts rejected than to report every unsuccessful book manuscript, and we may well suppose that this kind of oversight also had something to do with creating a discrepancy between editors' estimates and scholars' reports of manuscripts submitted. Proceeding on this assumption, and following our precedent in dealing with book manuscripts, we may conclude from the scholars' questionnaires that articles in English and American Literature confront the greatest difficulties in finding publication, followed by those in Philosophy and American History—an inference that is strengthened when we recognize that they also lag behind articles in other fields in rate of acceptance by journals published in the United States. (On the other hand, if we state domestic acceptances as a proportion of all submissions, articles in French Language and Literature fare equally badly with articles in English and Philosophy. American History had no for-

[5] In Economics 88 per cent of 147 article manuscripts was accepted; in Comparative Literature and in Medieval and Renaissance Literature, respectively, 76 per cent and 95 per cent of the small number of articles reported by faculty members holding appointments in English or American Literature. The exact figures for other fields of scholarship will be found in Appendix A.

eign submissions.) Finally, when we consider how large a proportion of the total number of scholarly manuscripts in Philosophy, and to a lesser extent of those in French, consists of articles rather than books, and that a number of acceptances in Philosophy required the authors to purchase reprints, we have still more evidence that publication is distinctly a problem in the former area and quite possibly a problem in the latter. In any event there seems to be no reason to doubt that some problems exist, albeit on a relatively minor scale, and nothing in the scholars' data seriously conflicts either with the statement of publishing difficulties we have developed by other means or with the proposals for eliminating them that are set forth in what follows.

Clearly learned journals are the most appropriate vehicle for studies that are impossible to print as articles but that do not warrant book-length publication even in monograph form. What is needed is funds to support publication of journal supplements in which single manuscripts of awkward length (or, in rare cases, groups of manuscripts reaching a difficult length but deserving simultaneous publication) may be printed as independent titles. From both a financial and an editorial point of view the journal supplement is very nearly an ideal solution to the problem of manuscripts of this description, and even scholarly authors may be expected to approve of the device when they cannot find publication in more usual form. It may also be an excellent vehicle for the occasional doctoral dissertation that cannot meet present-day tests of university press publication as a book and cannot qualify for inclusion in a monograph series, yet deserves a wider publication than microfilm and interlibrary loans afford. The form of the journal supplement would be particularly appropriate, moreover, if it is true that the important elements of most dissertations can be stated effectively in seventy-five or one hundred pages of type.

The economics of journal supplements are relatively simple when compared with those of full-fledged books. Any such book, for example, whether cloth-bound or paper-bound and whether large or small, creates editorial overhead for its publisher and is sold at a discount ranging for this type of study from a low of 10 per cent to an average of perhaps 20 per cent to a high of possibly 40 per cent. Editorial overhead and discounts both have the effect of raising the list price of any title, to which must also be added some small allowance for advertising in suitable channels. By this means the final product becomes far more costly than its actual printing costs, and even then it has no assured circulation. Were journals to publish occasional essay supplements, however, both the costs and the hazards of publication might be sharply reduced. In many cases the necessary editorial tasks might be absorbed without additional cost by the existing staff; there would be no need for discounts because distribution would take place by direct mail; and advertising could take the form of notice in the pages of a journal to its customary readers and subscribers, who would also be the most likely audience for such supplements as the editors undertook to publish.

Of course it would not do to "solve" the problems that essays of intermediate length create simply by burdening existing journals beyond their means. Hence the attitudes toward supplemental publication that editors representing a large number of different disciplines expressed in writing or in person have particular relevance here. In general, they either volunteered or responded sympathetically to the idea that special funds should be made available in aid of printing occasional journal supplements. Spokesmen for History were particularly eager to see devised some scheme of supplemental publication, but only one group of editors was wholly unenthusiastic, and even individual editors who were critical of the idea for various practical reasons suggested that if the difficulties they anticipated could be satisfactorily worked out they too would welcome the opportunity to publish essays they cannot now accommodate.

Among historians, for instance, one editor thought that the task of editing monographs in addition to standard journal articles would prove too taxing, and wondered as well why the necessary pages might not be incorporated into the journal itself rather than bound separately, but two other editors volunteered that a monograph supplement is the only feasible way to handle essays of undoubted merit but intermediate length, while five out of a total of six editors who commented on the question in interviews felt that occasional supplements would not add significantly (or at least excessively) to their usual burdens. Furthermore, two historical journals reported previous experience with occasional supplements, which the editors firmly believe to be an important vehicle for certain kinds of manuscripts, and they have abandoned them as a general policy only because of a shortage of funds, not of time.

Similarly, several editors of journals devoted to literature or one of the modern languages believe that the journal supplement would be an ideal vehicle for studies that cannot fit into the pages of a single journal but that should not be expanded into book form. Again one editor asked why the extra pages might not be incorporated into the regular pages of a journal, but he was outnumbered by others who see positive advantages in an independent vehicle of publication, and he himself suggested one reason for separate publication in raising the objection that automatic distribution of supplements to all subscribers to a journal might be wasteful.[6] Indeed only in Classics did there seem to be a conspicuous lack of interest in the very idea of supplements—and that because of the large number of vehicles for essay publication that are open to classical scholars, not only the *Transactions* of the American Philological Association but also the classical series of several universities. Hence the idea seems worthy of prolonged exploration of ways and means, especially in view of the fact that the only plausible alternative solution to the problems of extended essay publication seems to be a further expansion of the monograph series sponsored by learned societies. This alternative would neither serve scholarly authors better nor offer greater economies of production, and might preferably be reserved for still more extended studies. Certainly funds might be made available experimentally, on an application basis, without committing reluctant journals to expand beyond the limits of their resources.[7]

[6] Such an objection has merit, however, in pointing out potential difficulties in the operation of a program of supplementary publication. Direct sales upon receipt of individual orders would cost something in clerical help, handling, and extra postage. Automatic distribution would simplify these matters but raise production and mailing costs, and it would not provide for nonsubscribers. A combination of the two techniques would be a still more expensive but possibly a preferable solution, especially in view of the fact that most journals already offer back issues for sale to nonsubscribers.

[7] Furthermore, it should be noted that librarians whom we consulted in the course of the inquiry offered no grave objections to journal supplements, provided only that they were treated as a numbered series by each journal so that bookkeeping would be simple.

The same technique of making special funds available in relatively small amounts and upon suitable application could also be used to meet the other problems of journal publication that editors and scholars describe, although it might be simpler and more effective in the long run to award undifferentiated funds to journals that present a realistic budget reflecting a multiplicity of special needs and purposes. Perhaps the question should be decided not solely on the grounds of convenience in administration, but rather on the basis of some kind of decision as to whether the crucial need is to make financially possible certain types of printing that now present difficulties, or to exercise a more general influence over scholarly publishing. It should be relatively simple, for example, to administer separate funds for various special costs of publishing (illustrations and extraordinary composition, space for longer articles and existing backlogs, additional features and services to scholars); but it might be preferable to offer energetic editors an unusual opportunity to devise their own programs of editorial improvement while still making possible awards in aid of more nearby pedestrian activities that also require support of some sort.

Undifferentiated funds might also provide a means of testing in practice the supposition of a handful of distinguished editors that more creative editing and publishing would help to increase the market for scholarly journals. Of course, extra funds might have the effect of making the widely read journals even better known without offering equal advantages to specialized publications, but all might benefit from the educational influence of the leaders. Similarly the indifference we have imputed to some editors might be increased by an invitation to be creative, but possibly the accessibility of funds for various purposes (especially if it were known to scholarly authors) would challenge rather than confirm such complacency as may exist. In general there are real hazards attached to the bolder plan, which may nonetheless seem the more promising way of meeting contemporary problems where they originate.

One major question has gone without consideration here, however: the extent to which publication economies might be achieved by printing most learned journals by photographic offset from unjustified typewritten copy. In some few instances, of course, near-printing is to be avoided if possible. Moreover, a number of editors report that they cannot alter the processes employed by the university presses that handle their printing, and others have discovered that although near-print would be cheaper than letterpress if they were just beginning to publish they cannot now economize by switching printers or processes. Furthermore, there are apparently some instances in which near-printing would actually cost more than letterpress even under truly competitive conditions, and, finally, some few editors at state universities are required by law to employ intrastate printers whatever they may cost. In other words there is a long list of reasons why many journals must appear in letterpress, entirely apart from the loss of subscribers that they might suffer if they adopted cheaper techniques.

Yet there is also a vigorous argument—most often put forward by young editors of young publications that are produced by near-print—to the effect that near-printing will almost invariably save money without losing subscribers. Although their view sometimes has the overtones of dogma, it is no less believable on that account than the equally obvious prejudice of traditionalists. Indeed it is probably fair to say that it is more believable, for the opponents of near-print do not generally convey a sense of direct experience of the alternatives, and the innovators at least have the advantage of having tried the supposedly inferior process. Clearly, however, such a complicated issue cannot be settled by an ACLS committee even after far more extensive investigation than has been possible up to now; but perhaps any awards body might justifiably require of editors applying for financial support a statement that they have scrupulously explored the possibility of employing near-print, and have deliberately rejected it, if indeed they have, for valid economic reasons. In the long run it seems probable that a number of journals may be forced into near-print as an alternative to crowding more and more letters on every page, and learned societies may help to dignify and also perhaps to accelerate the change. Yet even this kind of leadership may be undesirable, especially if it is likely that typewriter composition and offset printing together will soon cost as much at professional rates as the conventional techniques of letterpress. As with every other problem confronting this inquiry there is at least one imponderable for every question, at the end as at the beginning of the study.[8]

[8] We should also mention one other proposal, put forward by members of the American Folklore Society, for reducing the costs of producing scholarly journals by centralizing their publication in a single mammoth agency, in which standardized format and procedures, a large volume of printing, and careful scheduling of operations would eliminate the waste that afflicts contemporary journal publication. But experienced editors' objections to such a plan seem to us to outweigh its potential mechanical advantages, and in any event it would offer no advantages of any kind to journals already published by large presses or by their own university presses, or to those required by law to employ intrastate printers.

5.

Conclusions

Our survey of scholarly publishing points to three main conclusions. The first, and in some ways the most important, is the fact that scholarly publication is not and cannot realistically be expected to become self-supporting. In its present extent and quality it depends heavily upon the generosity of philanthropic foundations, colleges and universities, and private individuals who help in various ways to support the preservation and dissemination of the results of scholarly research.

The considerable extent of this support must be kept in mind in considering the second of our conclusions, that at the present time in most branches of the humanities and social sciences the uncomplicated scholarly manuscript of good quality can usually count upon early publication at no expense to its author. Certainly the information we have gathered does not support the view that vast numbers of good scholarly manuscripts are unable to find publication for economic reasons.

Our third conclusion, however, is equally significant: certain kinds of scholarly manuscripts present unusual difficulties to publishers and therefore run extra hazards in competing for available funds. Without assigning any a priority, we put them into the following categories:

1. The work of good scholarly quality that is nevertheless so specialized that it will be read only by an audience professionally interested in the same limited field of scholarship. We have called this kind of manuscript "esoteric" because it will be immediately useful to only a small number of specialists, although it may embody scholarship of considerable importance to a wider audience of scholars during a generation or more to come. In practical terms, whereas scholarly presses are geared to the production of

books that will sell at least 1000 or even 1500 copies, the esoteric work cannot be expected to sell more than 500 or at the most 800 copies. Our report explains why micropublication is usually inappropriate for such works.

2. The manuscript that is too long to be printed as an article in a scholarly journal and too short to make a viable book—that is, one that would occupy most or all of the quarterly number of a learned journal, although if published in book form it would come to considerably less than normal length. For obvious financial reasons having no bearing on the scholarly nature of such manuscripts university presses cannot afford to print them without doing harm to their other publishing operations. Thus brevity, which should be a virtue, becomes an actual handicap in seeking publication.

3. The scholarly work that must provide the reader with special materials, expensive to compose or to reproduce, in order to convey adequately the results of scholarship. Such materials include plates and illustrations in Archaeology and the History of Art, special symbols appropriate to Music and Linguistics, and foreign languages in works dealing with ancient or modern literatures. In general, any work of scholarship that requires difficult composition is likely to be a problem for its publisher.

4. The scholarly tool work, which although it is seldom an original contribution to knowledge is nevertheless needed by scholars in their research. On one hand, the carefully edited text or scholarly translation tends to be sacrificed in competition with other kinds of volumes, especially when funds must be found to cover the cost of preparation as well as of publication. On the other hand, the large-scale tool work (the annals, bibliography, collected papers, or annotated finding list) presents any scholarly publisher with a host of extraordinary financial difficulties.

5. The very long or multivolume work representing original research, which constitutes a disproportionately heavy burden on a university press.

In addition, many scholarly journals are confronted with one or more of the difficulties that also inhibit the publication of books. Journals are frequently financially unable to publish monograph supplements, although these might be the best way of dealing with scholarly manuscripts of intermediate length. They often lack funds to publish articles that involve difficult composition or require high-quality illustrations, and their space is frequently so limited that they exclude bibliographies and other scholarly tools for which their pages would be especially suitable vehicles. Furthermore, although most journals benefit from a number of hidden subsidies, several find it difficult to continue their operations even on a reduced scale, while others are unable to grow with the fields they represent or to eliminate the backlogs of accepted manuscripts that scholarship in those fields has already created.

Obviously there are obstacles to scholarly publication today which can be dealt with only by the provision of appropriately administered funds. Equally obviously, such assistance to publication as this report suggests must supplement and extend, rather than divert, funds already employed to support scholarly publishing; for even if the costs of publication were to remain constant, university presses and learned journals would continue to be hard pressed to meet the growing needs of contemporary scholarship. It is also clear that if colleges and universities that do not already sponsor scholarly publication were to assume part of the financial responsibility for the publication, by university presses and scholarly journals, of manuscripts written by members of their faculties, some of the difficulties we have described could be solved without great cost to any single institution. Nevertheless, institutional sponsorship of scholarly manuscripts, while it might solve a number of individual problems, could not deal effectively and impartially with the basic difficulties we have discussed. In the last analysis the health of scholarly publishing will depend upon the devoted services of the community of scholars and upon the generosity of one or more of the philanthropic foundations.

APPENDICES

APPENDIX A:
Answers to the Scholars' Questionnaire

| FIELD | REPLIES | | DOCTORAL DEGREES | | BOOK MANUSCRIPTS REPORTED | | MANUSCRIPTS ACCEPTED/MANUSCRIPTS SUBMITTED [a] | | | | | |
| | | | | | | | Manuscripts of All Kinds | | | Non-Ph.D. Manuscripts | | |
	No.	Percentage [b]	No.	Percentage	No.	Rate [c]	Abroad	U.S.	Total	Abroad	U.S.	Total
English	151	30	131	87	66	.44	3/3	46/63	49/66	2/2	29/37	31/39
							2/2	39/63	41/66	2/2	28/37	30/39
American History	55	36	46	84	37	.67	...	30/37	30/37	...	14/17	14/17
							...	24/37	24/37	...	11/17	11/17
European History	49		44	90	23	.47	1/1	18/22	19/23	1/1	12/15	13/16
							1/1	17/22	18/23	1/1	12/15	13/16
Political Science	60	34	57	95	57	.95	11/11	35/46	46/57	9/9	30/33	39/42
							11/11	33/46	44/57	9/9	28/33	37/42
Philosophy	43	43	38	88	10	.23	...	10/10	10/10	...	7/7	7/7
							...	9/10	9/10	...	6/7	6/7

French	37	18	34	92	12	.32	3/3 1/3	8/9 7/9	11/12 8/12	1/1 1/1	6/7 5/7	7/8 6/8
Classics	23	41	22	96	14	.61	1/2 1/2	11/12 10/12	12/14 11/14	1/1 1/1	6/7 5/7	7/8 6/8
Music	25	23	15	60	5	.20	1/1 0/1	4/4 3/4	5/5 3/5	... ...	2/2 2/2	2/2 2/2
Art	18	23	16	89	10	.56	2/3 2/3	6/7 5/7	8/10 7/10	2/2 2/2	4/5 3/5	6/7 5/7
Geography	18	21	12	67	15	.83	2/2 2/2	13/13 13/13	15/15 15/15	2/2 2/2	13/13 13/13	15/15 15/15
TOTAL	479	30	415	87	249	.52	24/26 20/26	181/223 160/223	205/249 180/249	18/18 18/18	123/143 113/143	141/161 131/161

[a] In each pair of fractions the upper fraction gives acceptances on every basis (i.e., outright acceptances, acceptances with author subsidy, acceptances still awaiting subsidy of some sort), while the second fraction is limited to acceptances without personal subvention or contingency of subsidy.

[b] Ratio between appropriate replies and probable distribution of questionnaires at thirty large institutions.

[c] Number of scholarly book manuscripts divided by number of scholars replying to the questionnaire.

71

MANUSCRIPTS ACCEPTED/MANUSCRIPTS SUBMITTED

FIELD	Ph.D. Manuscripts [a]			All Volumes of Research [b]			Non-Ph.D. Research Volumes		
	Abroad	U.S.	Total	Abroad	U.S.	Total	Abroad	U.S.	Total
English	1/1	17/26	18/27	1/1	19/31	20/32	1/1	7/10	8/11
	0/1	11/26	11/27	1/1	13/31	14/32	1/1	7/10	8/11
American History	...	16/20	16/20	...	21/28	21/28	...	6/9	6/9
	...	13/20	13/20	...	17/28	17/28	...	5/9	5/9
European History	...	6/7	6/7	...	7/11	7/11	...	1/4	1/4
	...	5/7	5/7	...	6/11	6/11	...	1/4	1/4
Political Science	2/2	5/13	7/15	3/3	12/22	15/25	2/2	9/11	11/13
	2/2	5/13	7/15	3/3	11/22	14/25	2/2	8/11	10/13
Philosophy	...	3/3	3/3	...	5/5	5/5	...	3/3	3/3
	...	3/3	3/3	...	4/5	4/5	...	2/3	2/3
French	2/2	2/2	4/4	2/2	5/5	7/7	1/1	4/4	5/5
	0/2	2/2	2/4	1/2	4/5	5/7	1/1	3/4	4/5
Classics	0/1	5/5	5/6	0/1	...	0/1	...	...	...
	0/1	5/5	5/6	0/1	...	0/1	...	...	...
Music	1/1	2/2	3/3	1/1	2/2	3/3	...	...	...
	0/1	1/2	1/3	0/1	1/2	1/3	...	...	...
Art	0/1	2/2	2/3	1/2	2/2	3/4	1/1	...	1/1
	0/1	2/2	2/3	1/2	2/2	3/4	1/1	...	1/1
Geography	...	...	...	1/1	3/3	4/4	1/1	3/3	4/4
	...	...	...	1/1	3/3	4/4	1/1	3/3	4/4
TOTAL	6/8	58/80	64/88	9/11	76/109	85/120	6/6	33/44	39/50
	2/8	47/80	49/88	7/11	61/109	68/120	6/6	29/44	35/50

[a] Manuscripts apparently derived from the doctoral dissertation or its equivalent, whether or not substantially revised.
[b] Full-length volumes reporting the results of original research.

FIELD	Ph.D. Research Volumes [a]			Scholarly Texts and Translations			Short Monographs [b]		
	Abroad	U.S.	Total	Abroad	U.S.	Total	Abroad	U.S.	Total
English	...	12/21	12/21	1/1	16/20	17/21	2/2	5/5	7/7
	...	6/21	6/21	0/1	15/20	15/21	2/2	5/5	7/7
American History	...	15/19	15/19	...	5/5	5/5	...	4/4	4/4
	...	12/19	12/19	...	3/5	3/5	...	4/4	4/4
European History	...	6/7	6/7	1/1	6/6	7/7	...	4/4	4/4
	...	5/7	5/7	1/1	6/6	7/7	...	4/4	4/4
Political Science	1/1	3/11	4/12	1/1	4/4	5/5	2/2	16/17	18/19
	1/1	3/11	4/12	1/1	4/4	5/5	2/2	15/17	17/19
Philosophy	...	2/2	2/2	...	...	...	...	3/3	3/3
	...	2/2	2/2	...	...	...	...	3/3	3/3
French	1/1	1/1	2/2	1/1	3/4	4/5	...	...	...
	0/1	1/1	1/2	0/1	3/4	3/5	...	...	...
Classics	0/1	...	0/1	1/1	5/6	6/7	...	3/3	3/3
	0/1	...	0/1	1/1	5/6	6/7	...	3/3	3/3
Music	1/1	2/2	3/3	...	2/2	2/2	...	...	...
	0/1	1/2	1/3	...	2/2	2/2	...	...	...
Art	0/1	2/2	2/3	...	2/2	2/2	1/1	1/2	2/3
	0/1	2/2	2/3	...	1/2	1/2	1/1	1/2	2/3
Geography	...	...	...	...	3/3	3/3	1/1	4/4	5/5
	...	...	...	...	3/3	3/3	1/1	4/4	5/5
TOTAL	3/5	43/65	46/70	5/5	46/52	51/57	6/6	40/42	46/48
	1/5	32/65	33/70	3/5	42/52	45/57	6/6	39/42	45/48

[a] Manuscripts apparently derived from the doctoral dissertation or its equivalent, whether or not substantially revised.
[b] Monographs in form other than book-length publication; so identified in the questionnaire.

MANUSCRIPTS ACCEPTED/MANUSCRIPTS SUBMITTED

FIELD	Manuscripts of Chapters			Article Manuscripts Reported		Manuscripts of Articles		
	Abroad	U.S.	Total	No.	Rate [a]	Abroad	U.S.	Total
English	1/1	4/5	5/6	286 [b]	1.89	23/26	163/217	186/243
	1/1	4/5	5/6			23/26	163/217	186/243
American History	...	...	...	82	1.49	...	67/82	67/82
	...	...	...			...	67/82	67/82
European History	...	1/1	1/1	57	1.16	12/13	42/44	54/57
	...	1/1	1/1			11/13	41/44	52/57
Political Science	5/5	3/3	8/8	105	1.75	14/15	78/90	92/105
	5/5	3/3	8/8			14/15	78/90	92/105
Philosophy	...	2/2	2/2	88	2.05	12/15	59/73	71/88
	...	2/2	2/2			12/15	54/73	66/88
French	...	...	...	56	1.51	12/13	37/43	49/56
	...	...	...			12/13	37/43	49/56
Classics	...	3/3	3/3	35	1.52	3/3	31/32	34/35
	...	2/3	2/3			3/3	31/32	34/35
Music	...	...	...	23	.92	3/3	19/20	22/23
	...	...	...			3/3	19/20	22/23
Art	...	1/1	1/1	27	1.50	6/6	21/21	27/27
	...	1/1	1/1			6/6	19/21	25/27
Geography	...	3/3	3/3	22	1.22	1/1	20/21	21/22
	...	3/3	3/3			1/1	20/21	21/22
TOTAL	6/6	17/18	23/24	781	1.63	86/95	537/643	623/738
	6/6	16/18	22/24			85/95	529/643	614/738

[a] Number of article manuscripts divided by number of scholars replying to the questionnaire.
[b] Scholars in English and American Literature reported a total of 286 articles, but 22 in Medieval or Renaissance Literature and 21 in Comparative Literature are excluded from the tabulation of manuscripts submitted and accepted.

Acceptances of Scholarly Manuscripts by Type of Publisher

FIELD	FULL-LENGTH BOOK MANUSCRIPTS [a]									MANUSCRIPTS OF ARTICLES		
	All Manuscripts			Non-Ph.D. Manuscripts			Ph.D. Manuscripts [b]					
	Trade Presses	University Presses [c]	Foreign Presses	Trade Presses	University Presses [c]	Foreign Presses	Trade Presses	University Presses [c]	Foreign Presses	Quarterly Reviews and Magazines [d]	Learned Journals	Foreign Journals
English	12	23	2	10	12	1	2	11	1	12	151	23
American History	5	21	0	4	7	0	1	14	0	26	41	0
European History	6	7	1	5	2	1	1	5	0	1	41	12
Political Science	5	11	4	5	8	3	0	3	1	0	78	14
Philosophy	0	5	0	0	3	0	0	2	0	1	58	12
French	1	7	3	1	5	1	0	2	2	0	37	12
Classics	1	4	1	1	3	1	0	1	0	0	31	3
Music	2	2	1	2	0	0	0	2	1	0	19	3
Art	0	4	1	0	2	1	0	2	0	1	20	6
Geography	2	4	1	2	4	1	0	0	0	0	20	1
TOTAL	34	88	14	30	46	9	4	42	5	41	496	86

[a] Volumes of research, edited texts, and translations; not short monographs or chapters.

[b] Manuscripts apparently derived from the doctoral dissertation or its equivalent, whether or not substantially revised.

[c] "University presses" includes learned societies, museums, and similar agencies.

[d] Quarterly reviews of literature, quarterly journals of state historical societies, etc.

APPENDIX C:
University Presses That Provided Information for Our Inquiry

Antioch Press
The Catholic University of America Press
Columbia University Press
Cornell University Press
Duke University Press
Harvard University Press
Indiana University Press
The Johns Hopkins Press
Louisiana State University Press
Loyola University Press
Princeton University Press
Rutgers University Press
Stanford University Press
Syracuse University Press
University of California Press
University of Chicago Press
University of Florida Press
University of Georgia Press
University of Hawaii Press
University of Illinois Press
University of Kansas Press
University of Kentucky Press
University of Michigan Press
University of Minnesota Press
University of Nebraska Press
University of New Mexico Press
University of Oklahoma Press
University of Pittsburgh Press
University of the South Press
University of Texas Press
University of Virginia Press
University of Washington Press
University of Wisconsin Press
Wayne State University Press
The Press of Western Reserve University

APPENDIX D:
Answers to the Press Questionnaire

Information about both subsidized and unsubsidized books is grouped into columns representing the experience of a designated number of large university presses, middle-sized university presses, and small university presses, respectively, which are totaled in a fourth column and converted to percentage in a fifth. Numbers in parentheses refer to the number of presses from which figures in the column immediately below have been drawn.

In general, all of the presses reporting subsidized books are included in the larger number reporting unsubsidized books, although in some cases presses providing data on subsidized titles did not provide comparable data on unsubsidized works. In such cases, therefore, the figures given here are not strictly comparable, but they have been presented in this fashion in order to make maximum use of the detailed information available to us.

SUBSIDIZED BOOKS [a]					UNSUBSIDIZED BOOKS				

Elapsed Time Between Acceptance and Publication of Scholarly Books

	(7)	(8)	(7)	(22 Presses)		(7)	(11)	(9)	(27 Presses)	
Under 12 months	128	22	9	159	63%	102	45	21	168	59%
12 to 18 months	37	9	7	53	21	37	40	4	81	28
18 to 24 months	17	6	2	25	10	7	8	2	17	6
Over 24 months	10	6	0	16	6	14	7	0	21	7
TOTAL	192	43	18	253	100	160	100	27	287	100

First Printings of Scholarly Books

	(6)	(10)	(6)	(22 Presses)		(6)	(12)	(9)	(27 Presses)	
Under 400 copies	3	0	1	4	2%	1	1	1	3	1%
401–800 copies	30	11	1	42	20	15	3	3	21	7
801–1300 copies	27	23	8	58	27	23	20	0	43	15
1301–1800 copies	37	7	3	47	22	18	9	6	33	11
1801–2500 copies	25	13	2	40	19	27	28	8	63	22
Over 2500 copies	18	3	0	21	10	68	52	9	129	44
TOTAL	140	57	15	212	100	152	113	27	292	100

Discounts on Scholarly Books

	(5)	(9)	(6)	(20 Presses)		(4)	(10)	(7)	(21 Presses)	
Short discount	88	18	0	106	55%	49	10	1	60	28%
Trade discount	36	22	13	71	37	56	71	23	150	69
Other discount	7	5	3	15	8	2	5	0	7	3
TOTAL	131	45	16	192	100	107	86	24	217	100

[a] Subsidized books are those that made use of subventions provided by a philanthropic foundation, a learned society, a university department, or an individual scholar. They do not include books published upon the general operating funds of a press, even when granted by the parent university.

| | SUBSIDIZED BOOKS | | | | | UNSUBSIDIZED BOOKS | | | | |

Royalties on Scholarly Books [a]

	(6)	(8)	(6)	(20 Presses)		(6)	(11)	(8)	(25 Presses)	
No royalty	94	19	5	118	61%	21	33	4	58	20%
After N copies	26	13	7	46	24	51	25	15	91	32
On all copies	16	11	2	29	15	74	55	8	137	48
TOTAL	136	43	14	193	100	146	113	27	286	100

Sales of Scholarly Books
During a Period of from 7 to 24 Months

	(5)	(6)	(5)	(16 Presses)		(5)	(6)	(8)	(19 Presses)	
Under 400 copies	24	10	5	39	28%	16	4	1	21	13%
400–800 copies	41	13	5	59	43	15	13	9	37	22
801–1300 copies	21	7	0	28	20	23	13	6	42	25
1301–1800 copies	2	4	0	6	4	20	2	5	27	16
1801–2500 copies	2	1	0	3	2	10	6	0	16	10
2501–3500 copies	0	0	0	0	...	4	2	1	7	4
Over 3500 copies	2	0	0	2	1	11	2	4	17	10
TOTAL	92	35	10	137	98	99	42	26	167	100

Sales During 7 to 24 Months
as a Proportion of First Printings

	(4)	(6)	(5)	(15 Presses)		(4)	(6)	(8)	(18 Presses)	
Up to 30%	18	4	1	23	19%	16	7	4	27	18%
31%–50%	30	12	7	49	40	24	23	8	55	36
51%–70%	23	12	1	36	29	15	10	7	32	21
Over 70%	9	6	1	16	13	14	18	7	39	25
TOTAL	80	34	10	124	101	69	58	26	153	100

Expected Period in Stock for Scholarly Books

	(4)	(10)	(7)	(21 Presses)		(4)	(11)	(9)	(24 Presses)	
Under 2 years	0	1	0	1	1%	0	5	0	5	2%
2–5 years	9	7	3	19	12	2	26	7	35	15
5–10 years	53	32	7	92	56	51	56	12	119	52
Over 10 years	27	17	8	52	32	45	19	8	72	31
TOTAL	89	57	18	164	101	98	106	27	231	100

[a] Only payments made to authors are included in these figures, not returns made to financial sponsors of scholarly volumes.

APPENDIX E:
Learned Journals That Provided Information for Our Inquiry

Art and Architecture

    Art Bulletin
    College Art Journal
    Journal of Aesthetics and Art Criticism
    Journal of the Society of Architectural Historians

Classics and Archaeology

    American Journal of Archaeology
    American Journal of Philology
    Archaeology
    Berytus
    Classical Philology
    Transactions and Proceedings of the American Philological
       Association

Folklore

    American Journal of Folklore
    Midwest Folklore
    Southern Folklore Quarterly
    Western Folklore

General and Interdisciplinary

    American Quarterly
    Bucknell Review
    Ethics
    Journal of the American Oriental Society
    Journal of Asian Studies
    Journal of Near Eastern Studies
    New England Quarterly
    Political Science Quarterly
    Slavic and East European Journal
    Speculum
    Traditio
    Victorian Studies

History

American Historical Review
Hispanic-American Historical Review
Isis
Journal of Economic History
Journal of the History of Ideas
Journal of Modern History
Medievalia et Humanistica
Mississippi Valley Historical Review
Pacific Historical Review
Renaissance News
Studies in the Renaissance
William and Mary Quarterly

Modern Literatures and Languages—General

American Literature
Comparative Literature
The Journal of English and Germanic Philology
Modern Fiction Studies
Modern Language Notes
Modern Language Quarterly
Modern Philology
Nineteenth-Century Fiction
PMLA
Philological Quarterly
Romance Philology
Studies in Philology

Modern Literatures and Languages—Specialized

French Review
Germanic Review
Hispanic Review
Italica
Monatshefte
Romanic Review
Yale French Studies

Music

> Journal of the American Musicological Society
> Journal of Music Theory

Philosophy

> Journal of Philosophy
> Philosophical Review
> Philosophical Studies
> Philosophy and Phenomenological Research
> Review of Metaphysics

Social Sciences

> American Economic Review
> American Journal of Sociology
> American Sociological Review
> Journal of Political Economy
> Quarterly Journal of Economics

Other Journals

> Journal of Biblical Literature
> Language
> Publications of the American Dialect Society